Optimizing LLM Applications

Strategies for Speed and Efficiency for Real World

George Anvil

Table of contents

Dear Readers,

Your thoughts matter to us! If this book brought a smile or a moment of respite, please consider sharing your experience through a review. Your feedback is invaluable in making our books even more enjoyable for fellow tech and programming enthusiasts.

Thank you for your support!

Chapter 1. Introduction

Language Model Applications (LLMs) have reshaped how we interact with technology, but unlocking their full potential requires us to navigate the realm of speed and efficiency.

1.1 The Significance of Optimizing LLM Applications

Language Model Applications (LLMs) have woven themselves into the fabric of modern technology, revolutionizing the way we interact with machines and transforming industries across the board. However, while LLMs hold incredible promise, their raw power often remains latent without strategic optimization. This section delves deep into the pivotal role that optimization plays in unlocking the true potential of LLM applications.

At the core of LLMs lies their ability to process and understand human language. They decipher nuances, context, and intent, making them indispensable tools for tasks such as text generation, language translation, sentiment analysis, and even chatbots. Yet, their complexity comes at a cost: resource-intensive computations and demanding memory requirements.

Optimization isn't merely a technical luxury; it's a necessity. The significance of optimizing LLM applications can be observed from several angles:

1.1.1 Enhancing User Experience

The speed at which an LLM-powered application processes requests and generates responses is directly linked to user satisfaction. Imagine an AI-powered customer support chatbot that responds with almost imperceptible delays. Such responsiveness doesn't just increase user engagement; it also imparts a sense of reliability and efficiency to the application. By optimizing LLMs, we create applications that feel intuitive, fluid, and seamlessly integrated into users' experiences.

1.1.2 Reducing Resource Footprint

LLM applications can be resource hogs, demanding significant processing power and memory. Unoptimized applications might suffer from slow response times, sluggishness, or even crashes, particularly when faced with a high volume of concurrent requests. Optimization involves streamlining algorithms, memory management, and processing pipelines to reduce the application's resource footprint. This not only improves performance but also allows the application to serve a larger user base without overburdening the underlying infrastructure.

1.1.3 Enabling Real-World Deployments

The real world is dynamic and unpredictable. LLM applications must function efficiently across a range of scenarios, from handling sudden traffic spikes to delivering results in real-time. Optimizing these applications equips them to excel in real-world conditions, ensuring that they maintain high performance levels even during peak usage periods. This adaptability opens doors for LLM applications in critical areas such as emergency response, financial analysis, and live translations.

1.1.4 Driving Innovation

Innovation is a cornerstone of technological progress. Optimized LLM applications provide a fertile ground for pushing the boundaries of what's possible. When the computational overhead is minimized, developers can experiment with novel features, more complex algorithms, and richer user interactions. The ability to innovate and iterate rapidly becomes a key differentiator, propelling applications from being mere tools to becoming cutting-edge solutions.

In essence, optimizing LLM applications isn't just about squeezing out a bit more speed; it's about crafting applications that have a tangible impact on users, businesses, and industries. It's about unleashing the latent capabilities of LLMs, transforming them from impressive concepts into real-world powerhouses. As we journey deeper into this exploration, we'll uncover strategies, techniques, and insights that empower us to harness the full significance of optimizing LLM applications.

1.2 Navigating the Real-World Landscape of Speed and Efficiency

In the realm of technology, where milliseconds can make the difference between success and frustration, navigating the complex landscape of speed and efficiency is paramount. The real world is far from the controlled environments of labs and simulations. It's a dynamic ecosystem where LLM applications are put to the test, facing challenges ranging from diverse user behaviors to resource limitations. This section delves into the multifaceted aspects of this real-world landscape and how optimizing LLM applications within it requires a holistic approach.

1.2.1 The Heterogeneous User Landscape

Users are the lifeblood of any LLM application. However, these users come with a wide array of behaviors, preferences, and expectations. Some might seek rapid responses, while others might require more comprehensive analyses. An optimized LLM application must cater to this diversity, seamlessly accommodating varied input styles, languages, and usage patterns. Navigating this landscape involves crafting algorithms that strike a balance between precision and speed, ensuring that user experiences remain consistently high regardless of usage nuances.

1.2.2 Scalability Challenges

LLM applications often find themselves in scenarios where they must handle varying loads of user requests. Be it a sudden influx of traffic during a product launch or spikes in usage during peak hours, scalability is a concern. Navigating this challenge requires architectural decisions that allow the application to gracefully scale up or down based on demand. Techniques such as load balancing, distributed processing, and efficient data storage become crucial in creating applications that can thrive under different workloads.

1.2.3 Latency Matters

The impatient nature of modern users has put latency in the spotlight. Whether it's a chatbot, a language translation tool, or an AI-assisted writing platform, delays in responses can lead to disengagement. In the real world, even fractions of a second matter. Navigating this landscape involves optimizing every layer of the application stack, from network communication to algorithm execution. Techniques like caching, asynchronous processing, and predictive analytics play a pivotal role in minimizing latency.

1.2.4 Resource Constraints

Resources like processing power, memory, and network bandwidth aren't limitless. Optimizing LLM applications for the real world requires a judicious allocation of these resources. Striking the right balance between maximizing performance and conserving resources is a delicate task. This involves techniques like memory pooling, dynamic resource allocation, and on-the-fly compression, all geared towards ensuring that applications can operate efficiently even under resource constraints.

1.2.5 Security and Privacy

In the real world, security and privacy concerns are paramount. Users entrust LLM applications with their data, which must be handled responsibly. Navigating this landscape involves implementing encryption, authentication, and authorization mechanisms to safeguard user information. Balancing security measures with performance considerations is a fine art, ensuring that users' data is protected without compromising application speed and efficiency.

In conclusion, navigating the real-world landscape of speed and efficiency isn't a linear journey; it's a multidimensional challenge that demands a comprehensive understanding of user behaviors, system architectures, and performance optimization techniques. As we traverse this landscape in the subsequent chapters, we'll uncover strategies that empower us to not only navigate but conquer the real-world challenges, ensuring that our optimized LLM applications flourish in the dynamic and demanding environments they are destined for.

Chapter 2. Understanding LLM Applications

In this chapter, we embark on a journey to decode the complex world of Language Model Applications (LLMs). We'll unravel what makes them tick, exploring their inner workings and the role they play in modern technology. From there, we'll transition into understanding the real-world challenges that surround optimizing their performance.

2.1 Decoding Language Model Applications

Imagine a system that can not only comprehend the nuances of human language but respond in kind, generating text that aligns with context, tone, and intent. LLMs are the engines that drive this transformative capability, enabling machines to understand and generate human-like text. At the heart of LLMs are neural networks designed to unravel the intricacies of language and provide machines with the ability to communicate intelligently.

At the core of an LLM lies the concept of embeddings. These are numerical representations of words that allow machines to process and manipulate text data. By encoding words as vectors in high-dimensional space, embeddings capture semantic relationships between words, such as synonyms and antonyms. This enables LLMs to understand the meanings and associations behind the words they encounter.

However, grasping language goes beyond individual words. Context is crucial for understanding intent, and this is where attention mechanisms come into play. Attention mechanisms enable LLMs to focus on specific parts of a text, simulating the way humans pay attention to certain words in a sentence to make sense of the overall meaning. This mechanism allows LLMs to capture the nuances of context and construct coherent responses.

The transformer architecture serves as the backbone of many modern LLMs. Transformers facilitate long-range dependencies in text, allowing words that are distant from each other to influence one another's representations. This is pivotal for understanding the relationships between different parts of a text, resulting in more accurate and contextually rich language processing.

When an input sentence is fed into an LLM, the embeddings decode the words into vectors, the attention mechanisms identify relevant context, and the transformer architecture stitches these components together to generate a coherent output. This process mirrors the way humans understand and generate language, albeit at an immensely accelerated pace.

In summary, decoding language model applications is about understanding how these neural networks break down language into components, interpret context, and synthesize responses. The synergy of embeddings, attention mechanisms, and transformer architectures transforms LLMs from abstract algorithms into powerful tools capable of comprehending and generating text that resonates with human communication patterns.

In the upcoming sections, we will transition from understanding the intricacies of LLMs to delving into the challenges posed by real-world scenarios. By unraveling these complexities, we will lay the groundwork for the optimization strategies that await us.

2.2   Real-World   Challenges   in Performance Optimization

The allure of LLMs is undeniable, yet the real world is a stage with unpredictable lighting. The challenges we encounter are as diverse as the users they cater to, and they beckon us to rethink traditional optimization strategies. Here, we confront a mosaic of complexities that shape our journey:

2.2.1 Computational Demand

At the heart of LLMs lies their ability to comprehend and generate human-like language. This process involves complex computations that scale with the model's size and depth. As LLMs evolve to process more nuanced language patterns and complex semantics, their computational hunger grows exponentially.

Real-world LLM applications often face a dichotomy. On one hand, they must provide swift responses to user queries, demanding rapid computations. On the other hand, they encounter tasks that require extensive processing, such as language translations or generating lengthy text passages. This disparity creates a balancing act that requires optimizing LLMs for both speed and complexity.

Optimization Strategies for Computational Demand

In the quest for efficiency, several strategies emerge:

1. Parallel Processing: Harnessing the power of multiple processor cores or threads to distribute computational tasks can significantly speed up LLM operations. Techniques like data parallelism and model parallelism allow different parts of an LLM to be processed concurrently.

2. Batch Processing: Bundling multiple inputs into batches for simultaneous processing can enhance efficiency. Batching minimizes the overhead of loading data and reduces the number of redundant calculations, making LLMs work smarter.

3. Hardware Acceleration: Specialized hardware like GPUs and TPUs can dramatically accelerate LLM computations due to their architecture optimized for matrix operations, a cornerstone of neural networks.

4. Quantization: Reducing the precision of numerical values used in computations (like using 16-bit instead of 32-bit floating point) can cut down on computational demand while maintaining acceptable accuracy.

5. Model Pruning: Trimming redundant connections or parameters from the LLM architecture reduces computational complexity without severely impacting performance.

6. Caching: Storing previously computed results and reusing them when relevant can eliminate redundant calculations and reduce computational load.

Code sample for Computational demands;

```
import multiprocessing

def process_text(text):
    # Perform language processing on the given text
    return processed_text

if __name__ == '__main__':
    texts = ['Hello', 'How are you?', 'Goodbye']

    with multiprocessing.Pool(processes=2) as pool:
```

```
    processed_texts = pool.map(process_text,
texts)

    print(processed_texts)
```

2.2.2 Memory Hungry

The processing prowess of LLMs comes at a cost—consumption of memory resources. LLMs require substantial memory to store model parameters, intermediate computations, and input data. As models grow in size and complexity, the challenge of managing memory becomes increasingly critical.

Real-world LLM applications operate in diverse environments with varying memory constraints. From edge devices with limited RAM to cloud servers with abundant resources, optimizing memory usage ensures consistent performance across the spectrum.

Optimization Strategies for Memory Efficiency

Mitigating memory hunger involves strategic techniques:

1. Data Structures: Employing memory-efficient data structures reduces overhead. Techniques like sparse matrices and compressed representations help minimize memory consumption.

2. Memory Recycling: Recycling memory previously used by irrelevant data can free up resources for new computations, effectively reducing the overall memory footprint.

3. Dynamic Allocation: Allocating memory dynamically as needed and releasing it promptly prevents unnecessary memory usage.

4. Model Compression: Techniques like quantization and pruning reduce the memory needed to store model parameters without significantly affecting performance.

5. Memory Pools: Reusing memory blocks instead of frequently allocating and deallocating them can enhance efficiency by reducing memory fragmentation.

6. Streamlining Intermediate Data: Discarding or aggregating intermediate computations that are no longer needed prevents memory bloat during extended processing.

Code Sample on Memory efficiency;

```python
import numpy as np
from scipy.sparse import lil_matrix

# Create a dense matrix
dense_matrix = np.random.rand(1000, 1000)

# Create a sparse matrix
sparse_matrix = lil_matrix((1000, 1000))
for _ in range(10000):
    i, j = np.random.randint(0, 1000),
np.random.randint(0, 1000)
    sparse_matrix[i, j] = np.random.rand()
```

```
print("Dense matrix size:", dense_matrix.nbytes /
1024, "KB")
print("Sparse matrix size:",
sparse_matrix.data.nbytes / 1024, "KB")
```

2.2.3 The Latency Paradox

In the realm of real-time interactions, where every millisecond counts, the latency paradox looms large as a challenging adversary. Real-world Language Model Applications (LLMs) often need to generate responses swiftly without compromising the quality of their output. Navigating this conundrum forms a core aspect of optimizing LLM performance.

Optimizing Latency: Strategies and Considerations

1. Batching: Aggregating multiple input requests into a single batch can amortize computational overhead and reduce the overall response time, benefiting real-time applications.

2. Asynchronous Processing: Separating tasks into asynchronous workflows enables parallel execution, minimizing idle time and improving response times.

3. Predictive Loading: Anticipating user interactions and preloading relevant models or data can drastically reduce the perceived latency.

4. Caching: Storing and reusing previous responses can effectively eliminate recalculations, leading to quicker responses for recurring queries.

5. Dynamic Resource Allocation: Allocating computational resources based on demand allows LLMs to scale up when needed, ensuring rapid responses during peak usage.

Code Sample on latency;

```
import asyncio

async def process_text(text):
```

```
    # Simulate processing time
    await asyncio.sleep(1)
    return "Processed: " + text

async def main():
    texts = ['Hello', 'How are you?', 'Goodbye']
    tasks = [process_text(text) for text in texts]

    processed_texts = await asyncio.gather(*tasks)
    print(processed_texts)

asyncio.run(main())
```

2.2.4 Diversity of User Behaviors

The real-world landscape of Language Model Applications (LLMs) is a tapestry woven with diverse user behaviors, demands, and expectations. Navigating this tapestry presents a unique set of challenges that require nuanced optimization strategies.

Understanding the Challenge

Users interact with LLM applications in myriad ways. Some pose succinct queries, while others engage in lengthy conversations. Diverse language patterns, context switches, and variations in language proficiency further complicate the scenario. Optimizing for this diversity means creating LLMs that respond accurately and rapidly to a broad spectrum of inputs.

Strategies for Accommodating Diversity

1. Polyglot Flexibility: Crafting LLMs that handle multiple languages seamlessly requires robust multilingual capabilities. This involves language-specific fine-tuning, diverse training data, and careful consideration of language intricacies.

2. Contextual Adaptability: Adapting to shifts in context during a conversation is pivotal. Techniques like contextual embeddings and memory-augmented models allow LLMs to maintain coherent interactions over extended dialogues.

3. Variable Length Handling: LLMs must gracefully handle both short queries and lengthy texts without compromising response times. Techniques such as dynamic batching and efficient attention mechanisms are employed to ensure rapid yet contextually relevant outputs.

4. Quality-Quantity Balance: Striking the right balance between generating detailed responses and swift interactions is essential. This entails optimizing response generation algorithms to generate coherent text within the temporal constraints.

Code on Polyglot Flexibility Example:

```
from transformers import
AutoModelForCausalLM, AutoTokenizer

def generate_response(prompt, language="en"):
    model_name = f"turing/mt-natsec-{language}"
# Replace with an actual model name
```

```python
    model = AutoModelForCausalLM.from_pretrained(model_name)
    tokenizer = AutoTokenizer.from_pretrained(model_name)

    input_ids = tokenizer.encode(prompt, return_tensors="pt")
    output = model.generate(input_ids, max_length=50, num_return_sequences=1)

    response = tokenizer.decode(output[0], skip_special_tokens=True)
    return response

english_response = generate_response("Hello, how are you?")
spanish_response = generate_response("Hola, ¿cómo estás?", language="es")

print("English response:", english_response)
print("Spanish response:", spanish_response)
```

2.2.5 Security and Privacy Conundrums

In the evolving landscape of Language Model Applications (LLMs), where user data is both the fuel and concern, optimizing performance must go hand in hand with safeguarding security and privacy. This section delves into the complex dance between LLM optimization and the imperative to protect user information.

The Balancing Act

LLMs often deal with sensitive user data, from personal conversations to confidential information. Optimization strategies must ensure that performance enhancements don't compromise security and privacy. Striking this balance is non-negotiable in a world where data breaches can have far-reaching consequences.

Ensuring Security in Optimization

1. Encryption on the Wire: Utilizing secure communication protocols like HTTPS ensures that

data transmitted between users and the LLM application remains encrypted and protected from eavesdropping.

2. Secure Storage: Protecting data at rest by encrypting stored information prevents unauthorized access even if the physical storage is compromised.

3. Authentication and Authorization: Implementing robust authentication mechanisms prevents unauthorized access to LLM interfaces, ensuring that only legitimate users can interact with the application.

4. Privacy-Preserving Techniques: Techniques like differential privacy and federated learning allow LLMs to learn from user data while minimizing the risk of exposing personal information.

Respecting User Privacy

1. Data Minimization: Collecting only the minimum necessary data required for LLM operation reduces the potential risk associated with storing user information.

2. Anonymization: Removing or encrypting personally identifiable information from user data before processing adds a layer of privacy protection.

3. User Consent: Implementing clear consent mechanisms ensures that users are aware of how their data will be used and gives them control over their information.

Code sample on security;

```python
from cryptography.fernet import Fernet

# Replace with your actual encryption key
encryption_key = Fernet.generate_key()
cipher_suite = Fernet(encryption_key)

def encrypt_data(data):
    return cipher_suite.encrypt(data.encode())

def decrypt_data(encrypted_data):
```

```
                                      return
cipher_suite.decrypt(encrypted_data).decode()

sensitive_info = "This is sensitive information."
encrypted_info = encrypt_data(sensitive_info)
decrypted_info = decrypt_data(encrypted_info)

print("Original:", sensitive_info)
print("Encrypted:", encrypted_info)
print("Decrypted:", decrypted_info)
```

Optimizing for computational demand involves distributing tasks efficiently, using parallel processing where possible, and leveraging hardware accelerators such as GPUs to speed up calculations. In scenarios where low latency is crucial, thoughtful resource allocation and optimization of model parameters are essential.

Understanding the computational demand of LLMs is vital when aiming to optimize their performance. As we progress, we'll uncover more strategies to navigate this challenge, ensuring that the power of LLMs is harnessed effectively even in resource-intensive scenarios.

Chapter 3. Profiling and Analysis Techniques

In the pursuit of optimizing Language Model Applications (LLMs), the path forward becomes clearer when we have the ability to peer into their inner workings. This chapter equips us with the tools and techniques to dissect the performance of LLMs, unravel bottlenecks, and dive deep into the complex details that shape their behavior.

3.1 Unveiling Performance Bottlenecks

Imagine a puzzle with pieces scattered across a vast table. Each piece represents a segment of your LLM application's execution. Unveiling performance bottlenecks involves piecing together this puzzle to reveal patterns and outliers. Let's delve into the process:

The Role of Profiling Tools

Profiling tools serve as observatories that allow us to peer into the runtime behavior of our LLM applications. They provide detailed metrics on various aspects of execution, such as:

- Execution Time: Profilers measure how much time each function or method takes to execute. This helps us identify functions that consume a significant portion of time and might be candidates for optimization.

- Memory Usage: Monitoring memory usage helps pinpoint memory-intensive sections of the code, helping us optimize memory allocation and deallocation strategies.

- Function Calls: Profilers track the number of times each function is called, helping us identify functions that might be invoked more frequently than necessary.

Using Profiling Tools

One commonly used profiling tool in Python is `cProfile`, which comes bundled with the standard library. Here's a basic example of using `cProfile`:

```python
import cProfile

def expensive_function():
    result = 0
    for _ in range(1000000):
        result += 1
    return result

def main():
    for _ in range(10):
        expensive_function()

if __name__ == '__main__':
    profiler = cProfile.Profile()
    profiler.enable()

    main()

    profiler.disable()
```

```
profiler.print_stats(sort='cumulative')
```

Interpreting the Insight

Profiling tools empower us to make data-driven decisions about where to focus our optimization efforts. By analyzing the metrics provided by profiling tools, we can uncover performance bottlenecks, distinguish resource-intensive functions, and gain a comprehensive understanding of how our LLM application behaves during runtime.

2. Sampling and Tracing

1. Sampling: Imagine taking periodic snapshots of a moving object. Sampling, in the context of profiling, operates similarly. Profilers take periodic snapshots of your application's state during execution. By analyzing these snapshots, we can identify which functions are being executed, how frequently they're invoked, and where time is being spent.

2. Tracing: Tracing is akin to recording every step of a journey. Profilers that use tracing capture a detailed log of every function call, its parameters, and its duration. This method provides a complex view of the entire execution path, helping us understand the flow of execution and detect areas of inefficiency.

Using Sampling and Tracing

Python's `cProfile` provides both sampling and tracing capabilities. Here's a glimpse of how they work:

```python
import cProfile

def expensive_function():
    result = 0
    for _ in range(1000000):
        result += 1
    return result

def main():
    for _ in range(10):
        expensive_function()
```

```
if __name__ == '__main__':
    profiler = cProfile.Profile()
    profiler.enable()

    main()

    profiler.disable()

    # Profiling using sampling
        profiler.print_stats(sort='cumulative')    #
Sampling

    # Profiling using tracing
    profiler.dump_stats('tracing_results.prof')   #
Tracing
```

Sampling and tracing offer us different perspectives on the execution of our LLM application. Sampling helps us identify hotspots where execution spends the most time. Tracing, on the other hand, provides a comprehensive narrative of how functions interact, revealing the entire journey of execution.

Understanding Hotspots

1. Execution Time Distribution: Profilers reveal how much time each function or method consumes during execution. Functions with higher accumulated execution time are potential hotspots.

2. Cumulative Time: Profiling tools often display cumulative time, which includes both the time spent within a function and the time spent in the functions it calls. Functions with higher cumulative time are likely hotspots.

3. Call Counts: Frequent function calls can contribute to overall execution time. Even if a single call is fast, numerous calls can accumulate. Functions with high call counts are worth investigating.

Using Profiling Tools to Identify Hotspots

Python's `cProfile` and other profiling tools can help identify hotspots. Here's how you can do it:

```python
import cProfile

def expensive_function():
    result = 0
    for _ in range(1000000):
        result += 1
    return result

def main():
    for _ in range(10):
        expensive_function()

if __name__ == '__main__':
    profiler = cProfile.Profile()
    profiler.enable()

    main()

    profiler.disable()
```

```
profiler.print_stats(sort='cumulative') #
Identify hotspots
```

Identifying hotspots shines a light on the areas where optimization efforts can yield the most significant improvements. By focusing on optimizing functions with high cumulative time or frequent calls, you can effectively target the bottlenecks that impact your LLM application's performance the most.

The Art of Method-Level Analysis

1. Function Calls and Timing: Profilers track the number of times each function is called and the time spent within it. This information helps identify functions that might be invoked excessively or those that consume a disproportionate amount of time.

2. Nested Function Analysis: Functions often call other functions. Method-level analysis unveils the execution hierarchy, enabling us to understand the relationships

between different functions and identify potential inefficiencies in nested calls.

3. Parameter Impact: Analyzing how parameters affect function performance can be enlightening. Are certain parameter values causing functions to be slower? Method-level analysis can provide answers.

Using Profiling Tools for Method-Level Analysis

Python's `cProfile` and other profiling tools can be harnessed for method-level analysis. Here's how you can gain insights into function-level performance:

```python
import cProfile

def expensive_function():
    result = 0
    for _ in range(1000000):
        result += 1
    return result

def main():
```

```python
for _ in range(10):
    expensive_function()

if __name__ == '__main__':
    profiler = cProfile.Profile()
    profiler.enable()

    main()

    profiler.disable()
    profiler.print_stats(sort='time')  # Method-level
analysis by execution time
```

Method-level analysis reveals the nuances of function behavior, allowing us to uncover areas where optimization can have a profound impact. By focusing on individual methods, we can implement targeted optimizations, refactor inefficient sections, and ensure that every brushstroke contributes to the brilliance of the LLM application's performance.

3.2 In-Depth Analysis with Profiling Tools

In the quest to optimize Language Model Applications (LLMs), the journey often takes us into the complex realm of profiling tools—an arsenal of instruments that illuminate the dark corners of code execution. In this section, we dive deep into the world of in-depth analysis, leveraging these tools to dissect LLM performance, understand intricacies, and craft targeted optimizations.

The Role of Profiling Tools

Profiling tools are the surgeon's tools of the software world, allowing us to perform delicate operations on our codebase. These tools help us examine the runtime behavior of our LLM applications, revealing details that are vital for optimization:

1. Execution Time Profiling

This technique serves as a magnifying glass that allows us to scrutinize how much time different portions of our code consume during runtime. By delving into execution time profiling, we gain the ability to pinpoint bottlenecks, identify performance-hungry functions, and make informed decisions about optimization strategies.

Decoding Execution Time Profiling

1. Quantifying Function Execution Time: Execution time profiling involves measuring the time taken by each function to complete its task. Profilers collect data on function execution durations, offering a clear picture of which functions contribute most significantly to the overall execution time.

2. Identifying Hotspots: Profiling tools highlight functions that consume a significant portion of the execution time. These functions, often referred to as "hotspots," are prime candidates for optimization, as enhancing their efficiency can lead to substantial performance improvements.

3. Fine-Tuning Optimization Efforts: By identifying functions with the highest execution times, you can focus your optimization efforts on areas that promise the most impactful results. This targeted approach ensures that you maximize the return on your optimization investments.

Using Profiling Tools for Execution Time Profiling

Python's `cProfile` and other profiling tools provide the means to perform execution time profiling. Here's how you can harness them to gain insights into your LLM application's performance:

```python
import cProfile

def expensive_function():
    result = 0
    for _ in range(1000000):
        result += 1
    return result
```

```python
def main():
    for _ in range(10):
        expensive_function()

if __name__ == '__main__':
    profiler = cProfile.Profile()
    profiler.enable()

    main()

    profiler.disable()
    profiler.print_stats(sort='cumulative') #
Analyze execution time
```

Execution time profiling is a beacon that guides us toward optimizing LLM performance. By understanding which functions consume the most time, we're equipped to make informed decisions about where to focus our optimization efforts. Through this meticulous analysis, we transform sluggish sections of code into agile performers, enhancing the overall efficiency of our LLM applications.

2. Memory Usage Profiling

Memory usage profiling is a critical technique in the optimization journey of Language Model Applications (LLMs). It's akin to shining a spotlight on the often-overlooked aspect of memory management. This method allows us to scrutinize how memory is allocated, utilized, and released during the execution of our applications. By diving into memory usage profiling, we gain invaluable insights that help us optimize memory allocation, detect memory leaks, and ensure efficient memory utilization.

Understanding Memory Usage Profiling

1. Memory Allocation Patterns: Memory usage profiling unveils the patterns of memory allocation within your LLM application. It identifies which functions or segments of code are responsible for allocating memory, shedding light on the memory distribution across your application.

2. Tracking Memory Deallocation: Profiling tools not only uncover memory allocation but also track how and when memory is deallocated. This information is crucial for spotting areas where memory might not be effectively released, which could lead to memory leaks over time.

3. Optimizing Memory Efficiency: Armed with memory usage insights, you can strategically optimize memory allocation. This involves selecting appropriate data structures, reusing memory where possible, and minimizing unnecessary memory allocations.

Leveraging Profiling Tools for Memory Usage Profiling

Profiling tools like Python's `cProfile` can be extended to perform memory usage profiling. Here's a practical example to showcase the process:

```python
import cProfile

def memory_intensive_function():
    data = [0] * 1000000
```

```python
    return sum(data)

def main():
    for _ in range(10):
        memory_intensive_function()

if __name__ == '__main__':
    profiler = cProfile.Profile()
    profiler.enable()

    main()

    profiler.disable()
    profiler.print_stats(sort='memory')  # Analyze
memory usage
```

Deriving Insights for Efficient Memory Management

Memory usage profiling is akin to wielding a magnifying glass to scrutinize the hidden corners of your LLM application's performance. By gaining an understanding of memory allocation and deallocation patterns, you can identify memory-intensive functions, refine your memory management strategies, and ensure your LLM application is optimized not just for execution time, but also for memory efficiency.

3. Call Graphs and Hierarchy

Understanding the complex web of function interactions within Language Model Applications (LLMs) is a cornerstone of optimization. Call graphs and hierarchies provide a visual roadmap of these interactions, helping us decipher execution paths, identify performance bottlenecks, and choreograph the orchestration of our LLM applications for peak efficiency.

Deciphering Call Graphs and Hierarchies

1. Visualizing Function Relationships: Call graphs graphically represent how functions within your LLM application call each other. This visualization highlights the connections and flow of execution, making it easier to comprehend the complex web of interactions.

2. Spotting Performance Bottlenecks: Analyzing call graphs reveals functions that receive multiple calls or are deeply nested in the hierarchy. These functions can be potential bottlenecks that impact performance, guiding us toward areas that need optimization.

3. Mapping Execution Flow: Call hierarchies map out the sequence of function calls, showing which functions are invoked within other functions. This understanding illuminates how the execution flows through your application and offers insights into the cumulative behavior.

Leveraging Profiling Tools for Insightful Visualization

Tools like Python's `cProfile` extend their capabilities to visualize call graphs and hierarchies. Here's a hands-on example that showcases the process:

```python
import cProfile

def function_a():
    pass
```

```python
def function_b():
    function_a()

def main():
    function_b()

if __name__ == '__main__':
    profiler = cProfile.Profile()
    profiler.enable()

    main()

    profiler.disable()
    profiler.print_callers()  # Display call graph
```

Call graphs and hierarchies offer us a magnifying glass into the complex choreography of our LLM application's execution. By unraveling function relationships and understanding how they intertwine, we gain the power to optimize execution flow, address bottlenecks, and ensure that every function plays its part harmoniously in the symphony of LLM application performance.

4. Parameter Impact Analysis

In the journey of optimizing Language Model Applications (LLMs), understanding the influence of parameter values emerges as a crucial dimension. Parameter impact analysis allows us to dissect how varying parameter inputs affect the performance of our applications. This technique empowers us to make informed decisions, adapt our functions to diverse scenarios, and unlock the potential for finely-tuned LLM performance.

Exploring Parameter Impact Analysis

1. Varied Parameter Inputs: Parameter impact analysis involves experimenting with different values for input parameters. By systematically changing these values, we can observe how functions respond and measure their performance under varying conditions.

2. Identifying Optimal Values: Through analysis, we can pinpoint parameter values that lead to optimal performance. These values become our guidelines for real-world usage, ensuring that our LLM applications shine in a variety of scenarios.

3. Fine-Tuning Function Behavior: Armed with insights into parameter impacts, we can adapt functions to different scenarios. For example, we can adjust thresholds, boundaries, or configurations based on the best-performing parameter values.

Leveraging Profiling Tools for Parameter Impact Analysis

Profiling tools like Python's `cProfile` can be extended to perform parameter impact analysis. Here's an example that illustrates the process:

```
import cProfile

def function_with_parameter(parameter):
    result = 0
```

```python
    for _ in range(parameter):
        result += 1
    return result

def main():
    for i in range(1, 6):
        function_with_parameter(i)

if __name__ == '__main__':
    profiler = cProfile.Profile()
    profiler.enable()

    main()

    profiler.disable()
        profiler.print_stats(sort='cumulative')     #
Analyze parameter impact
```

Parameter impact analysis opens a door to dynamic optimization in LLM applications. By understanding how different parameter values impact performance, we gain the ability to fine-tune functions for diverse usage scenarios. This adaptability ensures that our LLM applications not only perform well in specific conditions but also thrive across a spectrum of real-world situations.

Chapter 4. Memory Management for Efficiency

This chapter delves into the art of memory management, providing insights into crafting ingenious data structures, sculpting memory footprints, and achieving real-world impact through optimal memory utilization.

4.1 Crafting Data Efficiency with Ingenious Structures

In the complex landscape of optimizing Language Model Applications (LLMs), memory efficiency is a prized gem that can be unearthed through the craft of designing ingenious data structures. This section delves deep into the art of data structure design, unraveling techniques that minimize memory consumption while preserving the functionality and performance of your LLM applications.

The Essence of Ingenious Data Structures

1. Redundancy Reduction in Data Structures

This strategy involves eliminating the wasteful duplication of data by storing shared or repeated information only once. By applying redundancy reduction techniques, we minimize memory consumption without compromising the integrity or performance of our LLM applications.

The Power of Redundancy Reduction

1. Shared Data Consolidation: In many LLM applications, data elements are shared across multiple instances. Redundancy reduction involves identifying such shared data and storing it centrally, rather than duplicating it for each occurrence. This approach significantly trims memory usage.

2. Index-Based Data Access: Rather than storing complete data items, we can store indexes that point to

a centralized repository. This is particularly effective when dealing with large datasets where data items are similar or duplicated across different contexts.

3. Caching Commonly Used Data: Redundancy reduction can be achieved through caching. Frequently used data can be cached in memory, reducing the need for repeated data storage and retrieval.

Practical Implementation of Redundancy Reduction

1. Example: Vocabulary Deduplication: In LLM applications, a vocabulary of words or tokens is often used. By creating a centralized vocabulary that stores unique words and then mapping text to these indexes, you can significantly reduce memory usage, especially when dealing with extensive text data.

2. Example: Shared Embeddings: In applications involving embeddings, multiple instances might share similar or even identical embeddings. Storing these embeddings centrally and referencing them through indexes reduces memory overhead.

3. Example: Deduplication using Hashing: Consider a scenario where your LLM application needs to store a large vocabulary of words. Redundancy often creeps in as multiple words might share common prefixes or suffixes. By using a hash-based deduplication approach, you can significantly reduce memory usage.

Code sample:

```python
class Vocabulary:
    def __init__(self):
        self.word_to_id = {}
        self.id_to_word = []

    def add_word(self, word):
        if word not in self.word_to_id:
            self.word_to_id[word] = len(self.id_to_word)
            self.id_to_word.append(word)

    def get_id(self, word):
        return self.word_to_id.get(word, -1)
```

```python
    def get_word(self, id):
        return self.id_to_word[id] if 0 <= id < len(self.id_to_word) else None

# Example usage
vocabulary = Vocabulary()
vocabulary.add_word("apple")
vocabulary.add_word("app")
vocabulary.add_word("bat")
vocabulary.add_word("batman")
vocabulary.add_word("apple")

print(vocabulary.get_id("apple"))  # Output: 0
print(vocabulary.get_id("bat"))    # Output: 2
```

In this example, the Vocabulary class employs hash-based deduplication to store unique words while maintaining their relationships with corresponding IDs. This efficient structure reduces redundancy and conserves memory by storing common prefixes or suffixes only once.

Redundancy reduction is a testament to the power of mindful data structure design. It's a strategy that allows us to craft LLM applications that are lean and efficient in memory usage. By identifying opportunities to store shared or repeated data centrally and utilizing indexing or caching, we achieve a delicate balance between memory efficiency and application functionality.

2. Compact Representations in Data Structures

This strategy revolves around designing data structures that use minimal memory while retaining the necessary information. By harnessing compact representations, we can significantly reduce memory consumption without compromising the core functionality or performance of our LLM applications.

The Essence of Compact Representations

1. Bitwise Operations: Compact representations often involve using bitwise operations to store multiple pieces of information within a single data unit. This technique leverages the fact that computers operate at

the binary level, allowing us to pack more information in fewer bits.

2. Variable-Length Encoding: For data with varying lengths, such as strings, variable-length encoding schemes can be employed. These schemes assign shorter codes to more frequent elements, effectively saving memory at the expense of encoding complexity.

3. Packed Arrays: Packed arrays utilize custom data structures that store elements in a space-efficient manner. These structures are tailored to minimize memory overhead while still allowing efficient access and manipulation of data.

Practical Implementation of Compact Representations

1. Example: Bit Vectors: In LLM applications that involve boolean flags or binary states, using bit vectors can save considerable memory. Each bit represents a true or false state, allowing you to store multiple boolean values within a single integer.

2. Example: Variable-Length Encoding for Strings: In scenarios where strings of varying lengths are prevalent, employing variable-length encoding schemes such as UTF-8 can lead to significant memory savings while accommodating various character lengths.

3. Example: Packed Arrays for Sparse Data: For applications dealing with sparse data, packed arrays can be employed to store only non-zero elements. This approach reduces memory usage without sacrificing the ability to access and manipulate data efficiently.

Efficiency through Ingenious Design

Compact representations underscore the art of balancing memory efficiency and functionality. By skillfully designing data structures that optimize memory usage through bitwise operations, variable-length encoding, or packed arrays, we ensure that our LLM applications are not only proficient in execution but also respectful of memory resources.

3. Tailored for LLM Applications: LLMs often have unique data requirements. Designing structures that align with these requirements is crucial. For example, sparse data representations, compressed formats for language models, and efficient ways of storing embeddings can drastically impact memory efficiency.

Leveraging Ingenious Structures in Practice

1. Example: Trie Data Structure: A trie is a tree-like data structure that's particularly efficient for storing strings. In an LLM application where word frequency matters, using a trie for vocabulary storage can lead to substantial memory savings.

2. Example: Compressed Sparse Row Matrix: For scenarios involving matrix operations like word embeddings or attention mechanisms, a compressed sparse row (CSR) matrix can be a memory-efficient choice. It stores only non-zero elements, making it ideal for sparse matrices.

3. Example: Variable-Length Encoding: When dealing with variable-length data, like text strings of different lengths, variable-length encoding schemes (e.g., UTF-8) can drastically reduce the memory required for character storage.

Here's a simple code example illustrating the concept of variable-length encoding using UTF-8 encoding for strings:

```
# Sample string data
strings = ["hello", "world", "optimization",
"techniques", "memory", "efficient"]

# Encode strings using UTF-8 variable-length
encoding
encoded_strings = [s.encode('utf-8') for s in
strings]

# Display original strings and their encoded
lengths
for i, s in enumerate(strings):
    encoded_length = len(encoded_strings[i])
```

```python
print(f"String: {s}\tEncoded Length: {encoded_length}")
```

In this example, the `encode` method with the `"utf-8"` encoding is used to convert each string into its variable-length UTF-8 encoded representation. Variable-length encoding allows different characters to be represented using varying numbers of bytes, optimizing memory usage.

Crafting data structures with memory efficiency in mind doesn't mean compromising functionality or performance. It's an art of balance that allows you to maximize the potential of your LLM applications while minimizing memory overhead. By applying the principles of ingenious structure design, you'll be well-equipped to create LLMs that shine both in execution and memory utilization.

4.2 Sculpting Memory Footprints for Real-World Impact

In the dynamic landscape of optimizing Language Model Applications (LLMs), memory footprint sculpting emerges as a powerful strategy that transcends mere technicality. This section delves deep into the art of sculpting memory footprints, showcasing how careful memory management can translate into tangible real-world impacts, enhancing both user experience and application performance.

Understanding Memory Footprint Sculpting

1. Optimization Beyond Technicality

Beyond the technical intricacies lies a facet of optimization that extends its influence to real-world impact. When we sculpt memory footprints, we're not merely reducing memory use. We're crafting Language Model Applications (LLMs) that operate swiftly and resonate with users. By minimizing memory consumption, we create applications that are more responsive, efficient, and accessible across devices.

This approach involves recycling memory, using resources judiciously, and managing object lifecycles. By reusing memory, objects, and smartly releasing resources, we build LLM applications that are not only technically proficient but also user-friendly and stable over the long run.

Key Takeaways:
- User Experience: Sculpted memory footprints lead to applications that respond quickly and offer seamless interactions, enhancing user satisfaction.
- Versatility: Optimized memory usage ensures your LLM applications can function smoothly across a range of devices, from modest hardware to high-performance systems.
- Stability: Effective memory management results in stable applications with fewer chances of memory-related issues, contributing to long-term reliability.

Sculpting memory footprints is more than code—it's a purposeful way of building LLM applications that leave a lasting impact on users and the real world they inhabit.

2. Reusing Memory Resources

Efficiency in memory management involves a clever approach: reusing memory. Instead of repeatedly creating and discarding memory, we recycle it whenever possible. By doing so, we reduce the need for constant memory allocation, making our Language Model Applications (LLMs) more resourceful and streamlined.

Why It Matters:
- Resource Conservation: Reusing memory reduces waste, conserving resources and contributing to optimized performance.
- Speed and Responsiveness: Memory reuse cuts down on the time spent creating and deleting memory, resulting in quicker and more responsive LLM applications.

- Memory Efficiency: Recycling memory minimizes memory churn, which is the process of frequent memory allocation and deallocation. This keeps memory usage in check.

Incorporating memory reuse in our LLM applications ensures we're not just saving memory, but also enhancing the overall efficiency and effectiveness of our software.

3. Lifecycle Management

In the realm of memory optimization for Language Model Applications (LLMs), lifecycle management plays a pivotal role. It's the art of efficiently handling the birth, life, and end of objects in your application.

What It Entails:
- Birth and Usage: Objects are created and put to work, serving their purpose within your LLM application.
- Efficient Usage: Objects are used effectively to carry out tasks without unnecessary memory overhead.

- Graceful Farewell: When objects are no longer needed, they're released from memory, preventing unnecessary memory consumption.

Why It's Important:
- Memory Efficiency: Effective lifecycle management ensures that memory is used efficiently throughout an object's existence.
- Preventing Leaks: Properly managing object lifecycles reduces the risk of memory leaks, which can lead to performance issues and instability.
- Stability and Performance: By managing the lifecycle of objects, you contribute to the overall stability and smooth performance of your LLM application.

Mastering lifecycle management ensures that your LLM application uses memory efficiently, stays stable, and performs optimally throughout its execution.

Strategies for Memory Footprint Sculpting

1. Pooled Resource Management: Implementing resource pools for frequently used objects allows you to

reuse memory, minimizing the overhead of creating and destroying objects repeatedly.

2. Object Recycling: Instead of constantly creating new instances of objects, consider reusing existing objects by resetting their states. This reduces memory churn and enhances application responsiveness.

3. Lazy Loading: Adopt a lazy loading approach, where resources are loaded only when they are required. This strategy prevents the unnecessary preloading of data and conserves memory.

Real-World Impact and Benefits

1. Enhanced User Experience: By sculpting memory footprints, you create LLM applications that respond swiftly and offer seamless interactions. Users appreciate applications that don't bog down their devices or waste resources.

2. Optimal Resource Utilization: Memory footprint optimization ensures that your LLM applications run

on a broader spectrum of devices, from resource-constrained devices to high-end systems.

3. Stability and Longevity: Effective memory management leads to stable applications with reduced chances of memory leaks or crashes, providing a solid foundation for long-term success.

Here's a simplified code sample demonstrating the concept of sculpting memory footprints by reusing memory resources and managing object lifecycles:

```python
class ResourcePool:
    def __init__(self, size):
        self.pool = [None] * size
        self.index = 0

    def get_resource(self):
        if self.index < len(self.pool):
            resource = self.pool[self.index]
            self.pool[self.index] = None
            self.index += 1
            return resource
        return None
```

```python
    def release_resource(self, resource):
        if self.index > 0:
            self.index -= 1
            self.pool[self.index] = resource

# Create a resource pool with a size of 3
pool = ResourcePool(3)

# Using and reusing resources
resource1 = pool.get_resource()
print("Resource 1:", resource1)

resource2 = pool.get_resource()
print("Resource 2:", resource2)

# Releasing resources
pool.release_resource(resource1)
pool.release_resource(resource2)

# Reusing released resources
reused_resource1 = pool.get_resource()
print("Reused Resource 1:", reused_resource1)

reused_resource2 = pool.get_resource()
print("Reused Resource 2:", reused_resource2)
```

In this example, the `**ResourcePool**` class demonstrates memory footprint sculpting by reusing resources. The pool allows you to get and release resources, reusing previously allocated memory. This approach reduces the need for repeated memory allocation and deallocation, resulting in a more efficient memory footprint.

Sculpting memory footprints transcends coding—it's about creating LLM applications with purpose and impact. By thoughtfully managing memory, you not only optimize technical aspects but also shape applications that resonate with users, delivering efficiency, responsiveness, and stability.

Chapter 5. Harnessing Parallelization and Concurrency

In the dynamic world of optimizing Language Model Applications (LLMs), the power of parallelization and concurrency emerges as a game-changer. This chapter delves into the realm of parallel execution and concurrent processing, showcasing how multi-threading and efficient concurrency strategies can maximize performance potential, creating LLM applications that excel in speed, efficiency, and real-world effectiveness.

5.1 Multi-threading: Maximizing Performance Potential

In the realm of optimizing Language Model Applications (LLMs), multi-threading emerges as a powerful technique that turbocharges performance by running multiple threads concurrently. Imagine threads as individual workers in your application, each executing tasks independently to achieve faster results. In this section, we delve into the world of multi-threading, exploring its mechanics, benefits, and challenges, as well as techniques to ensure smooth execution.

Understanding Multi-threading

1. Parallel Execution: Unlocking Simultaneous Power

Parallel execution is like assembling a team of workers to tackle tasks concurrently, speeding up the completion of projects. In the world of Language Model Applications (LLMs), it's like having multiple workers handle different parts of a task at the same time.

How It Works:

1. Task Splitting: Imagine a big task broken into smaller parts. In parallel execution, these parts are assigned to

different "workers" (threads), each independently working on their portion.

2. Simultaneous Progress: Threads work together, independently yet in harmony. While one thread crunches numbers, another might handle user interactions, allowing for faster overall progress.

3. Efficient Multi-Cores: Parallel execution shines on computers with multiple cores. Each core can handle a thread, resulting in more efficient utilization of the hardware.

Benefits in LLM Applications:

1. Speed Boost: Complex tasks, like processing large amounts of data, can be sped up significantly with parallel execution.

2. Responsive Interactions: While one thread handles heavy lifting, others keep interactions with users smooth and responsive.

3. Resource Efficiency: Utilizing multiple cores means your computer's resources are used more effectively, maximizing its potential.

Careful Management:

1. Thread Coordination: While threads work independently, they might need to share resources. Careful coordination is essential to avoid conflicts.

2. Data Consistency: When threads access shared data, ensuring consistency becomes important. Techniques like locks prevent chaos.

3. Balancing Act: Too many threads can lead to contention, reducing performance. Finding the right balance is crucial.

Parallel execution might sound complex, but it's like assembling a well-coordinated team to complete tasks together. By leveraging this technique, your LLM applications can achieve feats of efficiency and speed that were once unimaginable.

Here's a simple Python code sample that demonstrates parallel execution using the `concurrent.futures` module for multi-threading:

```python
import concurrent.futures

def process_data(data):
    result = data * 2  # Simulating some processing
    return result

data_to_process = [1, 2, 3, 4, 5]

# Using ThreadPoolExecutor for parallel execution
with concurrent.futures.ThreadPoolExecutor() as executor:
    # Submit tasks for processing
    futures = [executor.submit(process_data, data) for data in data_to_process]

    # Collect results as they complete
    results = [future.result() for future in concurrent.futures.as_completed(futures)]
```

```
print("Original Data:", data_to_process)
print("Processed Data:", results)
```

In this code sample, the `process_data` function represents some data processing task that takes a data value and returns a processed result. The `ThreadPoolExecutor` is used to submit tasks for processing in parallel using multiple threads. The results are collected as they complete, showcasing the concept of parallel execution.

Please note that Python's Global Interpreter Lock (GIL) limits the extent to which Python threads can achieve true parallelism. For CPU-bound tasks, consider using the `concurrent.futures.ProcessPoolExecutor` to leverage multi-processing.

2. Resource Sharing: Collaborative Memory Usage

Resource sharing is like a group of friends using a communal library—they share books, but they need to coordinate to avoid conflicts. In the realm of Language Model Applications (LLMs), it's about threads or parts of your program sharing memory and data, ensuring they work together without stumbling over each other.

Why It Matters:

1. Memory Conservation: Threads can share the same memory space, saving resources and preventing duplication.

2. Collaborative Tasks: Threads might need to work together on a task, requiring access to shared data for coordination.

3. Efficiency Gains: Sharing data allows threads to communicate and cooperate, achieving tasks more efficiently.

Challenges of Sharing:

1. Synchronization: Threads accessing shared data must synchronize their actions to prevent conflicts. This coordination ensures smooth collaboration.

2. Locking: Locks are like rules in the library—only one thread can "check out" data at a time. Others wait their turn to avoid confusion.

3. Balancing Act: While sharing is efficient, too much sharing can lead to bottlenecks and slower performance due to excessive synchronization.

Balancing Efficiency and Control:

1. Choose Wisely: Decide what data needs sharing and what should remain private to each thread.

2. Synchronize with Care: Use synchronization mechanisms like locks only when necessary to avoid unnecessary overhead.

3. Avoid Overuse: Don't make everything sharable. Consider if separate resources or isolated tasks might be better.

Resource sharing is about teamwork—threads collaborating to achieve tasks faster and more effectively. By sharing memory, you optimize resource usage, but a thoughtful balance between sharing and coordination is essential to ensure harmony in your LLM applications.

Here's a basic Python code sample illustrating resource sharing and synchronization using locks:

```python
import threading

# Shared counter variable
counter = 0

# Lock for synchronization
lock = threading.Lock()

def increment_counter():
    global counter
```

```python
    for _ in range(1000000):
        # Acquire lock before updating counter
        with lock:
            counter += 1

# Create multiple threads to increment the
counter
threads = []
for _ in range(5):
    thread = threading.Thread(target=increment_counter)
    threads.append(thread)
    thread.start()

# Wait for all threads to complete
for thread in threads:
    thread.join()

print("Final Counter Value:", counter)
```

In this example, multiple threads increment a shared `counter` variable. The `lock` ensures that only one thread can modify the counter at a time, preventing conflicts. By using a lock, you ensure that the shared resource is accessed safely, mitigating the risks associated with concurrent access.

Keep in mind that the example above focuses on demonstrating the concept of resource sharing and synchronization using locks. In practice, synchronization mechanisms should be used judiciously to balance efficiency and coordination in your Language Model Applications.

3. Concurrency Management: Orchestrating Harmony

Imagine a conductor leading an orchestra—a symphony of different instruments playing together. In the realm of Language Model Applications (LLMs), concurrency management is about orchestrating threads to work harmoniously, executing tasks simultaneously while maintaining order.

Why It's Important:

1. Task Diversity: Different threads might perform diverse tasks. Concurrency management ensures they cooperate without stepping on each other's toes.

2. Efficient Resource Usage: Managing threads effectively prevents overloading the system with too many tasks running concurrently.

3. User Experience: Concurrency keeps applications responsive by allowing multiple tasks to progress without causing delays.

Challenges and Strategies:

1. Synchronization: Threads accessing shared data need synchronization to avoid conflicts. Techniques like locks ensure orderly access.

2. Deadlocks: Threads waiting on each other indefinitely can lead to deadlocks. Avoiding circular waiting and using timeouts can help prevent this.

3. Task Division: Breaking tasks into smaller units that can run concurrently enhances performance and responsiveness.

Balancing Act:

1. Choose Concurrency Wisely: Not all tasks need concurrency. Balance between tasks that can be executed simultaneously and those that should run sequentially.

2. Avoid Overhead: Overusing concurrency management can lead to excessive synchronization, slowing down your application.

3. Testing and Tuning: Experiment with different levels of concurrency, monitor performance, and adjust as needed.

Concurrency management is like choreographing a dance—you want each thread to contribute its part without stepping on others' toes. By managing concurrency effectively, you create LLM applications that perform gracefully, optimizing tasks and delivering a seamless user experience.

Here's a basic Python code sample illustrating concurrency management using the `concurrent.futures` module to execute tasks concurrently:

```python
import concurrent.futures
import time

def process_task(task):
    print(f"Processing Task {task}")
    time.sleep(2)  # Simulating task execution
    print(f"Task {task} completed")

tasks = [1, 2, 3, 4, 5]

# Using ThreadPoolExecutor for concurrent execution
with concurrent.futures.ThreadPoolExecutor() as executor:
    # Submit tasks for processing concurrently
```

```
    futures = [executor.submit(process_task, task)
for task in tasks]

    # Wait for all tasks to complete
    concurrent.futures.wait(futures)

print("All tasks completed")
```

In this code sample, the `process_task` function represents a task that takes some time to complete. The `ThreadPoolExecutor` is used to execute tasks concurrently using multiple threads. The `submit` method is used to submit tasks for execution, and the `wait` function waits for all submitted tasks to complete.

This example demonstrates how concurrency management allows tasks to run concurrently, enhancing efficiency and responsiveness in your Language Model Applications.

Multi-threading Techniques

1. Thread Pools: Creating a pool of threads allows for efficient reusability, preventing the overhead of constantly creating and destroying threads.

2. Synchronization Mechanisms: Techniques like locks, semaphores, and mutexes help manage access to shared resources, ensuring data consistency.

3. Thread Safety: Designing thread-safe code ensures that multiple threads can access shared resources without causing conflicts.

While multithreading offers significant benefits, it requires careful design and management. Overusing threads can lead to complexity and reduced performance due to contention. Balancing the number of threads, optimizing tasks for parallelism, and thoughtful synchronization are key to harnessing multithreading potential effectively.

5.2 Concurrency Strategies for Real-World Efficiency

In the complex domain of optimizing Language Model Applications (LLMs), concurrency strategies act as powerful tools that go beyond mere speed. This section delves into a spectrum of techniques that enhance real-world efficiency through concurrency, catering to various scenarios and use cases.

Understanding Concurrency Strategies

1. Asynchronous Programming

Asynchronous programming is like managing a busy café—while waiting for one order to complete, you take another order. In the realm of LLMs, asynchronous programming allows tasks to overlap, making the most of time that would otherwise be wasted on waiting. This strategy is particularly valuable for I/O-bound tasks, such as fetching data from the internet.

2. Parallelism with Tasks

Parallelism is like distributing workload among a group of friends to finish a project faster. In LLM applications, you can use tasks to break down complex tasks into smaller units, executing them in parallel. This strategy benefits CPU-bound tasks, like intense calculations or data processing.

3. Event Loops

An event loop is like managing a conference—keeping track of speakers and sessions, ensuring each topic gets its time. In LLM applications, event loops help manage and prioritize tasks, ensuring efficient resource usage and responsiveness.

4. Thread Pools

Thread pools are like having a group of workers always ready to take on tasks. In LLM applications, maintaining a pool of threads allows for efficient task allocation and reuse, preventing the overhead of constantly creating and destroying threads.

5. Task Prioritization

Task prioritization is like organizing your to-do list, tackling the most important tasks first. In LLM applications, you can assign priority levels to tasks, ensuring that critical tasks get prompt attention while maintaining overall efficiency.

6. Resource Limitation

Resource limitation is like rationing supplies—you ensure each task gets its fair share of resources. In LLM applications, setting resource limits prevents any single task from hogging resources and affecting the entire system's performance.

Adapting to Real-World Scenarios

1. Tailored Approach

Different scenarios require different strategies. Asynchronous programming suits tasks waiting for external data, while parallelism shines for CPU-heavy calculations.

2. Hybrid Techniques

Combining strategies can yield optimal results. For example, using both asynchronous programming and parallelism can tackle tasks with varying characteristics.

3. Measurement and Adjustment

Experimentation and measurement are key. Monitor performance, adjust strategies, and fine-tune as needed to achieve the best balance.

Concurrency strategies elevate your LLM applications beyond mere execution, delivering real-world efficiency and responsiveness. By adopting and customizing these techniques, you craft applications that thrive in diverse scenarios, whether it's fetching data from the web, processing complex calculations, or handling a multitude of tasks gracefully.

Here's a Python code sample that demonstrates different concurrency strategies using the `asyncio` library for asynchronous programming and the `concurrent.futures` module for parallelism with tasks:

```python
import asyncio
import concurrent.futures

# Asynchronous programming using asyncio
async def fetch_data(url):
    print(f"Fetching data from {url}")
    await asyncio.sleep(2)  # Simulating data fetching
    print(f"Data from {url} fetched")

async def main_async():
    tasks = [fetch_data("https://example.com") for _ in range(3)]
    await asyncio.gather(*tasks)
```

```python
# Parallelism with tasks using
ThreadPoolExecutor
def process_task(task):
    print(f"Processing Task {task}")
    return task * 2

def main_parallel():
    tasks = [1, 2, 3]
    with concurrent.futures.ThreadPoolExecutor() as executor:
        results = list(executor.map(process_task, tasks))
    print("Processed Results:", results)

# Event loop for asynchronous programming
asyncio.run(main_async())

# Parallelism with tasks
main_parallel()
```

In this code sample, the `fetch_data` function represents an asynchronous task that simulates fetching data from a URL. The `main_async` function demonstrates asynchronous programming using the `asyncio` library.

The `process_task` function represents a CPU-bound task that processes data. The `main_parallel` function showcases parallelism using the `ThreadPoolExecutor` from the `concurrent.futures` module.

Please note that the code sample is for demonstration purposes and focuses on illustrating different concurrency strategies. In real-world applications, you might encounter more complex scenarios that require careful handling and fine-tuning of concurrency strategies.

Chapter 6. Algorithmic Excellence

In the realm of optimizing Language Model Applications (LLMs), algorithmic excellence is the cornerstone of efficiency and effectiveness. This chapter embarks on a journey into the world of advanced text processing algorithms, unraveling their potential to elevate LLM performance and deliver real-world results.

6.1 Elevating Text Processing Algorithms for Real-World Results

In the captivating domain of Language Model Applications (LLMs), the choice of text processing algorithms isn't just technical—it's the difference between good and exceptional. In this section, we embark on a journey that goes beyond algorithms' technicalities, exploring how strategic algorithmic selection and refinement can transform raw text into real-world results that dazzle users and enrich application outcomes.

The Art of Algorithmic Selection:

1. Problem-Specific Algorithms: Tailoring Precision to Purpose

Just as a tailor crafts clothes to fit perfectly, problem-specific algorithms are designed to match the nuances of a particular task. In the universe of Language Model Applications (LLMs), these algorithms are the tools that ensure your application performs exceptionally, as they are meticulously crafted to address the specific challenges of different tasks.

Why They Matter:

1. Precision Matters: Problem-specific algorithms are specialized, honed to excel in a particular task. They offer higher accuracy and reliability compared to general-purpose solutions.

2. Targeted Efficiency: Instead of applying a one-size-fits-all approach, these algorithms focus resources on the intricacies of the task at hand, making the most of your application's capabilities.

3. Diverse Applications: Language tasks vary widely—from language translation to sentiment analysis. Using problem-specific algorithms optimizes your LLM for specific applications.

Examples of Problem-Specific Algorithms:

1. Named Entity Recognition (NER): Algorithms designed for NER excel at identifying entities like names, dates, and locations in text—a crucial task for applications dealing with data extraction.

2. Part-of-Speech Tagging (POS): Algorithms specialized in POS tagging classify words in a sentence by their grammatical role. This is essential for tasks like syntactic analysis.

3. Text Summarization: Algorithms tailored for summarization identify key points in a text and generate concise summaries. They're invaluable for applications requiring content condensation.

Code Example: Part-of-Speech Tagging

Let's explore the world of Part-of-Speech tagging using the `nltk` library:

```
import nltk
from nltk import pos_tag
from nltk.tokenize import word_tokenize

nltk.download('punkt')

# Sample sentence
sentence = "The cat sat on the mat."

# Tokenize the sentence
tokens = word_tokenize(sentence)

# Perform Part-of-Speech tagging
```

```
pos_tags = pos_tag(tokens)

print("Part-of-Speech Tags:", pos_tags)
```

In this code snippet, we use the `nltk` library to apply
Part-of-Speech tagging to a sentence. This specialized
algorithm assigns grammatical roles to words, which is
crucial for applications requiring in-depth linguistic
analysis.

Problem-specific algorithms ensure that your LLM
applications don't merely understand text, but they
understand it in a way that's tailored to the task at hand.
This precision-driven approach is at the heart of
achieving superior results in real-world scenarios.

2. Performance Metrics: Quantifying Excellence

In the journey of optimizing Language Model
Applications (LLMs), performance metrics act as the
compass, guiding you toward algorithmic excellence.
These metrics are like measurements taken by a chef to
ensure a perfect dish—they quantitatively assess

algorithm performance, giving you insight into how well your LLM is meeting real-world demands.

Why They're Vital:

1. Objective Evaluation: Performance metrics provide an objective way to measure how well an algorithm is performing. They remove subjective bias and provide concrete evidence of success.

2. Comparison Benchmark: Metrics allow you to compare different algorithms or versions of algorithms. You can objectively identify which approach yields the best results.

3. User-Centric Focus: Ultimately, your LLM serves users. Performance metrics help you ensure that your application meets user expectations and delivers value.

Essential Performance Metrics:

1. Accuracy: Accuracy is like hitting a bullseye—how often an algorithm correctly predicts the outcome. It's

suitable for balanced datasets but may be misleading in imbalanced scenarios.

2. Precision and Recall: Precision is about being precise, even if you're not catching everything. Recall is about catching as many relevant instances as possible, even if there are some false positives.

3. F1-Score: The F1-score balances precision and recall. It's a harmonic mean of the two and is great for scenarios where you want to consider both false positives and false negatives.

Code Example: Evaluating Accuracy

Let's assess the accuracy of a simple classifier using the `sklearn` library:

```
from sklearn.metrics import accuracy_score
from sklearn.datasets import load_iris
from          sklearn.model_selection          import
train_test_split
```

```python
from sklearn.neighbors import KNeighborsClassifier

# Load Iris dataset
data = load_iris()
X, y = data.data, data.target

# Split data into training and testing sets
X_train, X_test, y_train, y_test = train_test_split(X, y, test_size=0.2, random_state=42)

# Create a KNeighborsClassifier
classifier = KNeighborsClassifier(n_neighbors=3)

# Fit the classifier and make predictions
classifier.fit(X_train, y_train)
predictions = classifier.predict(X_test)

# Calculate accuracy
accuracy = accuracy_score(y_test, predictions)
print("Accuracy:", accuracy)
```

In this code snippet, we use the `sklearn` library to train a K-Nearest Neighbors classifier and calculate its accuracy. Accuracy is a fundamental performance metric that indicates how often the classifier's predictions match the actual labels.

Performance metrics arm you with data-driven insights, guiding you toward algorithmic choices that deliver real-world results. By understanding and applying these metrics, you ensure that your LLM applications perform at their best and make a meaningful impact.

3. Customization and Hybridization: Tailoring Excellence

In the dynamic world of Language Model Applications (LLMs), customization and hybridization are the artists' palette, enabling you to craft algorithms that resonate with your specific needs. Like a skilled painter mixing colors for a unique shade, these strategies empower you to create algorithmic solutions that go beyond off-the-shelf options.

Why They Shine:

1. Precise Fit: Every LLM application has unique demands. Customizing algorithms allows you to fine-tune them to your application's specific challenges and intricacies.

2. Hybrid Vigor: Hybridization blends the strengths of multiple algorithms. By combining approaches, you harness the best of each, resulting in superior performance.

3. Adaptability: Customized algorithms adapt to your changing needs. As your application evolves, these algorithms can evolve with it, maintaining optimal performance.

Strategies for Customization and Hybridization:

1. Parameter Tuning: Customization begins with parameter adjustment. Fine-tune hyperparameters to optimize algorithm behavior for your specific use case.

2. Feature Engineering: Modify or create features that the algorithm uses for decision-making. Crafting features that align with your application's goals can significantly enhance performance.

3. Ensemble Methods: Hybridization often involves ensemble methods—blending predictions from multiple algorithms. Techniques like bagging and boosting combine outputs to improve accuracy and robustness.

Code Example: Ensemble Method (Bagging)

Let's explore bagging, an ensemble method, using the `sklearn` library:

```
from sklearn.ensemble import BaggingClassifier
from sklearn.tree import DecisionTreeClassifier
from sklearn.datasets import load_iris
from sklearn.model_selection import train_test_split
from sklearn.metrics import accuracy_score
```

```python
# Load Iris dataset
data = load_iris()
X, y = data.data, data.target

# Split data into training and testing sets
X_train, X_test, y_train, y_test = train_test_split(X, y, test_size=0.2, random_state=42)

# Create a base classifier
base_classifier = DecisionTreeClassifier()

# Create a BaggingClassifier
bagging_classifier = BaggingClassifier(base_classifier, n_estimators=10)

# Fit the classifier and make predictions
bagging_classifier.fit(X_train, y_train)
predictions = bagging_classifier.predict(X_test)

# Calculate accuracy
```

```
accuracy = accuracy_score(y_test, predictions)
print("Accuracy:", accuracy)
```

In this example, we use a bagging ensemble method to enhance the performance of a Decision Tree classifier. Bagging creates multiple versions of the base classifier, training them on different subsets of the data, and combines their predictions to achieve improved accuracy.

Customization and hybridization empower your LLM applications to transcend the ordinary. By tailoring algorithms to your application's unique needs and combining the strengths of multiple approaches, you create solutions that stand out and excel in real-world scenarios.

Fine-Tuning and Refinement:

1. Data Quality: The quality of training data greatly impacts algorithm performance. Clean, relevant, and diverse data ensures algorithms are well-prepared for real-world scenarios.

2. Hyperparameter Tuning: Algorithms have adjustable settings called hyperparameters. Tuning these parameters can optimize algorithm behavior for your specific use case.

3. Validation and Testing: Rigorous validation on different data sets and thorough testing reveal how algorithms perform in varied contexts, simulating real-world usage scenarios.

4. Sentiment Analysis

Let's explore sentiment analysis, a common LLM task, using the popular `**NLTK**` library:

```
import nltk
from         nltk.sentiment         import
SentimentIntensityAnalyzer

nltk.download('vader_lexicon')

# Initialize the sentiment analyzer
```

```python
sia = SentimentIntensityAnalyzer()

# Analyze sentiment of a sentence
sentence = "I love this product! It's amazing."
sentiment_scores = sia.polarity_scores(sentence)

# Interpret sentiment scores
if sentiment_scores['compound'] > 0.1:
    sentiment = 'Positive'
elif sentiment_scores['compound'] < -0.1:
    sentiment = 'Negative'
else:
    sentiment = 'Neutral'

print("Sentiment:", sentiment)
```

This code snippet demonstrates sentiment analysis using the `NLTK` library's `SentimentIntensityAnalyzer`. By selecting the right algorithm and fine-tuning its parameters, you can accurately gauge sentiment in text, a vital component for understanding user interactions.

Algorithmic excellence in text processing is more than a technical choice—it's a strategic decision that impacts user experience and application outcomes. By understanding the intricacies of algorithm selection, refinement, and customization, you pave the way for your LLM applications to deliver results that resonate in the real world.

6.2 Advanced Tokenization for Real-World Efficiency

In the complex tapestry of Language Model Applications (LLMs), tokenization is the thread that weaves meaning from text. Advanced tokenization techniques go beyond splitting text into words—they sculpt language into units that encapsulate context and meaning. This section unveils the world of advanced tokenization, demonstrating how it enhances real-world efficiency in understanding, processing, and interacting with text.

Understanding Advanced Tokenization:

1. Beyond Words: Sculpting Language's Essence

In the captivating world of Language Model Applications (LLMs), advanced tokenization goes beyond the confines of individual words. It's the artist's chisel, carefully shaping text into units that encapsulate a deeper linguistic essence. This section unravels the magic of advanced tokenization, exploring how it dismantles language barriers and elevates your LLM's understanding of context and meaning.

Going Deeper:

1. Phrases and Sub-phrases: Advanced tokenization doesn't stop at individual words—it identifies phrases that carry collective meaning. "New York City," for instance, is recognized as a unit that encapsulates a geographical entity.

2. Idiomatic Expressions: Expressions like "once in a blue moon" transcend literal meanings. Advanced

tokenization captures these idioms as singular entities, preserving their cultural significance.

3. Contextual Merging: Tokens fuse context with linguistic structure. Numbers, dates, and names are treated as holistic tokens, retaining their individual importance within the broader context.

Real-World Implications:

1. Nuanced Understanding: Advanced tokenization empowers your LLM to grasp language intricacies. It moves beyond mere words, deciphering phrases and expressions that carry layers of meaning.

2. Streamlined Processing: By recognizing larger units, your LLM expedites comprehension. Contextual awareness reduces the need for exhaustive analysis, enhancing processing efficiency.

3. Enhanced Communication: Applications can communicate more effectively by recognizing

multi-word units. This lends a human touch, allowing interactions to mirror natural conversations.

Code Example: Multi-Word Recognition

Let's explore advanced tokenization using the `nltk` library in Python:

```
import nltk
from nltk import word_tokenize

# Sample text
text = "Once in a blue moon, he makes a special appearance."

# Tokenize the text
tokens = word_tokenize(text)

print("Individual Tokens:", tokens)
```

In this code snippet, the `nltk` library's tokenization reveals individual tokens. However, advanced tokenization would encapsulate "once in a blue moon" as a single token, preserving the idiomatic expression's integrity.

Advanced tokenization is like unlocking a treasure trove of language—it bridges the gap between words and meaning, enriching your LLM's language comprehension. By venturing beyond words, you equip your applications to engage with text more holistically, nurturing a deeper connection with users.

2. Contextual Awareness: Illuminating Text's Essence

In the captivating realm of Language Model Applications (LLMs), contextual awareness is the beacon that guides algorithms to interpret text beyond its surface. Like a skilled interpreter deciphering cultural nuances, contextual awareness infuses meaning into tokens, allowing LLMs to grasp subtleties and depths that words alone can't convey. This section unveils the power of contextual awareness, showing how it enriches your LLM's understanding and interactions.

The Art of Contextual Awareness:

1. Capturing Significance: Contextual awareness imbues tokens with significance. Dates, numbers, and names aren't isolated; they're recognized as entities carrying relevance in the broader narrative.

2. Phrases as Wholes: Advanced tokenization fuses phrases into single units. Contextual awareness treats these units as coherent entities, preserving their collective meaning.

3. Domain Nuances: Specialized tokenizers attuned to specific domains recognize terms unique to those fields, ensuring domain-specific context is maintained.

Real-World Impact:

1. Elevated Interpretation: Contextual awareness bridges the gap between text and its intended meaning. Your LLM understands more than words—it grasps the intricacies woven within phrases.

2. Informed Decisions: Algorithms can make informed choices by comprehending the relevance of dates, names, and numbers, enhancing the accuracy of processing.

3. Intelligent Interactions: Applications engage users intelligently, recognizing idiomatic expressions and multi-word units for a more natural, human-like interaction.

Code Example: Named Entity Recognition

Let's delve into contextual awareness using Named Entity Recognition (NER) with the `spaCy` library in Python:

```
import spacy

# Load English NER model
nlp = spacy.load("en_core_web_sm")

# Sample text
```

```
text = "Apple Inc. was founded by Steve Jobs on
April 1, 1976."

# Process the text with spaCy
doc = nlp(text)

# Extract named entities
for entity in doc.ents:
        print("Entity:", entity.text, "    Type:",
entity.label_)
```

In this code snippet, the `spaCy` library's NER model identifies named entities like "**Apple Inc.,**" "**Steve Jobs,**" and "**April 1, 1976.**" Contextual awareness enables the model to recognize these entities and their significance within the text.

Contextual awareness is like unlocking a secret code—it reveals layers of meaning within text, enhancing your LLM's grasp of language subtleties. By infusing your applications with this awareness, you empower them to comprehend text beyond the surface, offering users interactions that reflect human understanding.

3. Specialized Tokenizers: Crafted for Domain Insight

In the complex landscape of Language Model Applications (LLMs), specialized tokenizers are the artisans that fashion language understanding with precision. Like expert translators navigating technical jargon, these tokenizers are tailored to specific domains, ensuring that your LLM interprets text with domain-specific nuances intact. This section unveils the prowess of specialized tokenizers, illustrating how they elevate domain-specific language comprehension.

Why Specialized Tokenizers Shine:

1. Domain Sensitivity: Specialized tokenizers are finely attuned to domain-specific vocabulary and language conventions. They interpret terms unique to the field, maintaining context accuracy.

2. Technical Jargon: Certain domains—like medicine or law—feature complex terminology. Specialized

tokenizers navigate this jargon, preserving meaning in technical contexts.

3. Cultural Nuances: Domain-specific applications often involve cultural references. These tokenizers safeguard idiomatic expressions and cultural terms, enhancing authenticity.

Real-World Applications:

1. Medical Texts: Specialized tokenizers in medical LLMs recognize medical terms, drugs, and procedures, ensuring accurate language processing in the medical domain.

2. Legal Documents: For legal LLMs, tokenizers navigate complex legal jargon, interpreting contracts, clauses, and legal concepts accurately.

3. Financial Analysis: Tokenizers in financial LLMs grasp financial terms, stock symbols, and market references, enabling nuanced analysis of financial texts.

Code Example: Medical Tokenization

Consider a simple example of medical tokenization using the `spaCy` library in Python:

```python
import spacy

# Load specialized medical tokenizer
nlp = spacy.load("en_core_sci_md")

# Sample medical text
text = "The patient was diagnosed with myocardial infarction."

# Process the text with the medical tokenizer
doc = nlp(text)

# Print medical terms
medical_terms = [token.text for token in doc if token.is_alpha and token.ent_type_ == "MEDICAL_CONDITION"]
print("Medical Terms:", medical_terms)
```

In this code snippet, the `spaCy` library's specialized medical tokenizer recognizes medical terms like **"myocardial infarction,"** demonstrating domain-specific understanding.

Specialized tokenizers empower your LLM applications to master domain intricacies. By embracing these tokenizers, you ensure that your applications interpret domain-specific text with accuracy, making them invaluable tools for niche contexts.

Benefits in Real-World Efficiency:

1. Enhanced Understanding: Advanced tokenization captures the essence of text, enabling LLMs to comprehend language nuances and deliver more accurate insights.

2. Efficient Processing: Tokens carry contextual meaning, reducing the need for extensive linguistic analysis. This accelerates processing while maintaining accuracy.

3. Improved Interactions: Applications can interact more intelligently by understanding multi-word expressions, idioms, and domain-specific terms.

Code Example: Multi-Word Tokenization

Let's explore a simple example of advanced tokenization using the `spaCy` library in Python:

```
import spacy

# Load English tokenizer, POS tagger, parser, and NER
nlp = spacy.load("en_core_web_sm")

# Sample text
text = "New York City is often called the Big Apple."

# Process the text with spaCy
doc = nlp(text)

# Print tokens and their POS tags
```

```
for token in doc:
    print("Token:", token.text, "    POS Tag:",
token.pos_)
```

In this code snippet, the `spaCy` library's advanced tokenizer processes a sentence, breaking it down into tokens along with their associated Part-of-Speech (POS) tags. The tokenizer identifies phrases like "New York City" as a single unit, demonstrating the advanced contextual awareness of tokens.

Advanced tokenization is like deciphering a complex puzzle—it transforms text into meaningful components that LLMs can navigate and understand. By employing advanced tokenization techniques, you infuse your applications with the ability to process text more efficiently and interact with users in a more intuitive and accurate manner.

Chapter 7. Caching and Preprocessing Strategies

In the realm of optimizing Language Model Applications (LLMs), efficiency isn't just about algorithms—it's also about strategic data management. This chapter unveils the power of caching and preprocessing strategies, demonstrating how they accelerate access to data, streamline processing, and elevate real-world application performance.

7.1 Data Caching: Accelerating Real-World Access

In the dynamic universe of Language Model Applications (LLMs), data caching emerges as a strategic ally. Imagine a library catalog—you store frequently accessed books on a shelf near the entrance for quick retrieval. Similarly, data caching involves storing frequently used data in a readily accessible location. This section delves into the intricacies of data caching, revealing how it accelerates real-world data access and bolsters the efficiency of your LLM.

Why Data Caching Matters:

1. Reduced Latency: Speeding Up Data Access

In the bustling world of Language Model Applications (LLMs), reduced latency acts as a turbocharger, propelling your applications toward faster and more responsive data access. Picture a high-speed train—you reach your destination quicker without unnecessary stops. Similarly, reduced latency minimizes the time it takes for data to travel from its source to your application, resulting in swifter interactions and improved user satisfaction.

The Power of Reduced Latency:

1. Instant Gratification: Reduced latency translates into quicker responses. Your LLM applications retrieve data faster, providing users with near-instantaneous results.

2. Seamless Interactions: Applications with low latency engage users in real-time conversations. Whether it's chatbots or information retrieval, the speed of interaction remains uninterrupted.

3. Enhanced User Experience: Faster data access means smoother navigation. Users experience seamless transitions between pages, enhancing overall satisfaction.

Strategies for Achieving Reduced Latency:

1. Caching: Store frequently used data closer to your application, minimizing the time required to fetch it from its original source. This is especially effective for data that doesn't change often.

2. Content Delivery Networks (CDNs): Utilize CDNs to distribute content across multiple servers globally. This ensures that users can access data from a server nearest to their location, reducing physical distance.

3. Optimized Queries: Efficiently structured database queries retrieve only the necessary data, reducing the time spent fetching irrelevant information.

Code Example: Using CDN for Image Delivery

Consider implementing a CDN for image delivery using a service like Cloudinary:

```html
<!-- Original Image URL -->
<img
src="https://example.com/images/my-image.jpg"
alt="My Image">

<!-- Image Delivered via CDN -->
<img
src="https://cdn.example.com/images/my-image.jp
g" alt="My Image">
```

In this example, the image is delivered via a CDN, ensuring that users access the image from a server that offers reduced latency, depending on their geographic location.

Reduced latency is like transforming your application into a high-speed vehicle—it zips through data access, delivering information to users with astonishing speed. By incorporating strategies that minimize latency, you create LLM applications that provide a fluid and seamless experience, keeping users engaged and satisfied.

2. Computational Relief: Easing Processing Strain

In the complex realm of Language Model Applications (LLMs), computational relief acts as a supportive ally, lightening the processing burden that algorithms bear. Picture a team of assistants helping with tasks—they share the workload, making operations smoother and more efficient. Similarly, computational relief reduces the strain on your LLM's processing capabilities, optimizing its performance and responsiveness.

The Essence of Computational Relief:

1. Efficiency Boost: Computational relief lessens the demand on processing resources, allowing your LLM to execute tasks with increased speed and efficiency.

2. Resource Allocation: By minimizing computational overhead, your LLM can allocate its resources to higher-priority tasks, enhancing overall application performance.

3. Scalability: Relief techniques ensure that as your application scales, processing demands remain manageable, ensuring consistent user experiences.

Strategies for Providing Computational Relief:

1. Caching: Store pre-calculated results or frequently used data, reducing the need to repeatedly perform complex calculations.

2. Parallelization: Distribute tasks across multiple processing units, allowing your LLM to tackle multiple tasks simultaneously, thus accelerating processing.

3. Optimized Algorithms: Choose algorithms that are optimized for specific tasks, reducing unnecessary computation and improving efficiency.

Code Example: Parallel Processing with `concurrent.futures`

Consider parallel processing using the `concurrent.futures` module in Python:

```python
import concurrent.futures

# Function to process data
def process_data(data):
    return data  2

data = [1, 2, 3, 4, 5]

# Use ThreadPoolExecutor for parallel processing
with concurrent.futures.ThreadPoolExecutor() as executor:
    results = list(executor.map(process_data, data))
```

```
print("Results:", results)
```

In this example, the `ThreadPoolExecutor` allows parallel processing of data, where each element is squared concurrently, providing computational relief by leveraging multiple threads.

Computational relief is like a safety net for your LLM—it prevents processing bottlenecks and ensures smooth performance. By adopting strategies that alleviate computation strain, you empower your applications to navigate tasks with agility and efficiency, delivering responsive and dependable user experiences.

3. Consistency Control: Ensuring Reliable Results

In the complex landscape of Language Model Applications (LLMs), consistency control is the guardian that ensures your applications provide reliable and accurate results. Imagine an orchestra playing in harmony—consistency control conducts the performance, ensuring that each instrument produces the right notes at the right time. Similarly, consistency control in LLMs safeguards data integrity, providing trustworthy outcomes across requests and interactions.

The Role of Consistency Control:

1. Data Integrity: Consistency control prevents conflicting or contradictory data from causing confusion. It maintains data accuracy and integrity, even in complex scenarios.

2. Reliable Outcomes: By enforcing consistent behavior, your LLM applications deliver dependable results, building user trust and confidence in their interactions.

3. Error Prevention: Consistency control minimizes errors arising from discrepancies between cached data and real-time updates, fostering seamless user experiences.

Strategies for Ensuring Consistency:

1. Cache Expiration: Define how long cached data remains valid. Regularly refresh the cache to prevent users from accessing outdated or incorrect information.

2. Cache Invalidation: Implement mechanisms to invalidate cached data when changes occur in the underlying data source. This ensures that users access the most recent information.

3. Transaction Management: When dealing with databases, use transactions to ensure that operations are executed completely or not at all, preventing partial or inconsistent updates.

Code Example: Cache Expiration with `cachetools`

Consider cache expiration using the `cachetools` library in Python:

```
from cachetools import TTLCache

# Create a cache with a maximum size of 100 items
and a TTL of 300 seconds
```

```python
cache = TTLCache(maxsize=100, ttl=300)

# Function to simulate data retrieval
def retrieve_data(key):
    # Simulate data retrieval
    print(f"Fetching data for key: {key}")
    return f"Data for {key}"

# Cache data retrieval with expiration
def cached_data_retrieval(key):
    if key in cache:
        return cache[key]
    else:
        data = retrieve_data(key)
        cache[key] = data
        return data

# Fetch data using caching
print(cached_data_retrieval("user_1"))
print(cached_data_retrieval("user_1"))  # Data is
retrieved from cache due to cache expiration
```

In this code snippet, the `TTLCache` from the `cachetools` library ensures that cached data has a defined expiration time (TTL). Once the TTL expires, the data is fetched again to maintain accuracy and consistency.

Consistency control is like a vigilant referee—it ensures that your LLM applications play by the rules and provide reliable outcomes. By implementing strategies that enforce data consistency, you create applications that users can depend on, cultivating an environment of trust and authenticity.

Implementing Data Caching:

1. In-Memory Storage: Store cached data in memory, which offers rapid retrieval due to its proximity to processing units. Libraries like `memcached` and `Redis` facilitate this.

2. Caching Policies: Decide how long data should be cached (cache expiration) or when to update the cache

(cache invalidation) based on data volatility and application requirements.

3. Key-Value Pairing: Associate cached data with unique keys for easy retrieval. When a request arrives, the application checks the cache using the key.

Code Example: Using `cachetools` Library

```
from cachetools import LRUCache

# Create an LRU cache with a maximum size of
100 items
cache = LRUCache(maxsize=100)

# Function to simulate data retrieval
def retrieve_data(key):
    # Simulate data retrieval
    print(f"Fetching data for key: {key}")
    return f"Data for {key}"

# Cache data retrieval
def cached_data_retrieval(key):
```

```python
    if key in cache:
        return cache[key]
    else:
        data = retrieve_data(key)
        cache[key] = data
        return data

# Fetch data using caching
print(cached_data_retrieval("user_1"))
print(cached_data_retrieval("user_2"))
print(cached_data_retrieval("user_1"))
```

In this code snippet, we use the `**LRUCache**` class from the `**cachetools**` library to implement caching. Data is retrieved and stored in the cache, reducing data retrieval overhead.

Data caching is like having frequently used tools right at your fingertips—it optimizes data access and enhances your LLM's responsiveness. By embracing caching, you ensure that your applications thrive in real-world scenarios, where speed and efficiency are paramount.

7.2 High-Impact Preprocessing for Real-World Applications

In the dynamic world of Language Model Applications (LLMs), preprocessing is the sculptor's chisel, shaping raw data into refined inputs that fuel efficient and accurate operations. Think of it as preparing ingredients before cooking—a chef's meticulous arrangement enhances the final dish. This section unveils the art of high-impact preprocessing, revealing how it optimizes your LLM's readiness for real-world challenges.

Understanding Preprocessing's Significance:

1. Raw to Refined: Transforming Data's Essence

In the complex realm of Language Model Applications (LLMs), the journey from raw to refined data is akin to refining gold from ore. Just as gold is hidden within rocky earth, valuable insights lie within unstructured data. Preprocessing—your LLM's refinement process—unlocks these insights by reshaping data into a structured and usable form. This section delves into the transformative power of preprocessing, showcasing how it enhances your LLM's ability to decipher and analyze data.

Unlocking Data's Potential:

1. From Chaos to Structure: Preprocessing molds unstructured text into a structured format, enabling your LLM to navigate and interpret data with precision.

2. Noise Eradication: Unwanted characters, symbols, or irrelevant terms—like distractions—diminish data quality. Preprocessing eliminates this noise, ensuring focus on meaningful content.

3. Setting the Stage: Just as a painter prepares a canvas, preprocessing lays the foundation for your LLM's algorithms to paint accurate and insightful interpretations.

Essential Preprocessing Techniques:

1. Text Normalization: Standardize text by converting it to lowercase and removing accents. This ensures consistency and uniformity in analysis.

2. Tokenization: Break text into individual tokens—words or phrases—enabling your LLM to process language at a granular level.

3. Stopword Removal: Omit common words—like "and," "the," "is"—that add little meaning but clutter analysis.

Code Example: Text Transformation

Explore text preprocessing using Python's `nltk` library:

```
import nltk
from nltk.corpus import stopwords
from nltk.tokenize import word_tokenize
from nltk.stem import WordNetLemmatizer
```

```python
# Sample text
text = "The quick brown foxes are jumping over
the lazy dog's back."

# Tokenization
tokens = word_tokenize(text)

# Remove stopwords
stop_words = set(stopwords.words("english"))
filtered_tokens = [word for word in tokens if
word.lower() not in stop_words]

# Lemmatization
lemmatizer = WordNetLemmatizer()
lemmatized_tokens =
[lemmatizer.lemmatize(token) for token in
filtered_tokens]

print("Original Tokens:", tokens)
print("Preprocessed Tokens:", lemmatized_tokens)
```

In this code, we showcase tokenization, stopword removal, and lemmatization—essentials in transforming raw text into refined and meaningful tokens.

The journey from raw to refined data is like sculpting a masterpiece from raw clay—it transforms data into a valuable asset, enhancing your LLM's abilities to understand, analyze, and interact with information. By embracing preprocessing, you infuse your applications with the finesse to tackle real-world challenges and extract insights that lie hidden within data's depths.

2. Noise Reduction: Refining Data's Harmony

In the complex world of Language Model Applications (LLMs), noise reduction is the conductor that orchestrates clarity within data. Picture a symphony—the conductor ensures that each instrument's harmony shines through, without interference. Similarly, noise reduction in LLMs removes unwanted elements—like static on a radio—allowing the true essence of data to emerge.

This section unveils the art of noise reduction, demonstrating how it enhances data quality and enriches your LLM's comprehension.

The Essence of Noise Reduction:

1. Distilling Clarity: Noise reduction eliminates irrelevant characters, punctuation, or words, ensuring that your LLM's focus remains on meaningful content.

2. Enhancing Signal: Just as noise masks a signal's clarity, data noise obscures valuable insights. Noise reduction reveals the signal within the noise.

3. Streamlining Analysis: Noise-free data streamlines analysis, enabling your LLM to interpret and process data more efficiently and accurately.

Strategies for Noise Reduction:

1. Stopword Removal: Common words like "and," "the," "is" add little value. By removing them, you retain

meaningful terms that contribute to data understanding.

2. Punctuation Removal: Extraneous symbols or punctuation can disrupt data flow. Removing them ensures that your LLM focuses solely on textual content.

3. Numeric Exclusion: For textual analysis, numbers often introduce noise. Omitting them simplifies data and supports text-centric understanding.

Code Example: Noise Reduction

Consider noise reduction using Python's `nltk` library:

```
import string
from nltk.corpus import stopwords
from nltk.tokenize import word_tokenize

# Sample text with noise
text = "The quick #brown foxes are jumping over
the lazy dog's back!"
```

```python
# Tokenization
tokens = word_tokenize(text)

# Remove stopwords and punctuation
stop_words = set(stopwords.words("english"))
filtered_tokens = [word for word in tokens if
word.lower() not in stop_words and word not in
string.punctuation]

print("Original Tokens:", tokens)
print("Noise-Reduced Tokens:", filtered_tokens)
```

In this code snippet, noise reduction is achieved by eliminating stop words and punctuation from the text, resulting in a more focused and clear set of tokens.

Noise reduction is like a restorative touch—it uncovers the authentic voice of your data, enabling your LLM applications to perceive data's true essence. By mastering noise reduction techniques, you elevate your applications to sift through data clutter, enabling them to focus on what truly matters—meaningful content and valuable insights.

3. Feature Engineering: Crafting Data's Gems

In the complex realm of Language Model Applications (LLMs), feature engineering is the artisan's workshop, where data's raw materials are transformed into exquisite gems of understanding. Picture a jeweler cutting, polishing, and setting precious stones to create dazzling jewelry—feature engineering similarly enhances data's value, crafting insights that illuminate your LLM's capabilities. This section explores the craft of feature engineering, revealing how it enriches your LLM's interpretation and analysis.

The Art of Feature Engineering:

1. Data Enrichment: Feature engineering creates new attributes from existing data, enriching your LLM's understanding and enabling it to capture more nuanced insights.

2. Domain Relevance: Tailored features capture domain-specific nuances, enabling your LLM to excel in tasks specific to certain industries or contexts.

3. Model Enhancement: By presenting data in a way that resonates with your LLM's algorithms, feature engineering optimizes model performance and prediction accuracy.

Essential Feature Engineering Techniques:

1. Textual Transformation: Converting text into numerical features using techniques like TF-IDF (Term Frequency-Inverse Document Frequency) or word embeddings.

2. One-Hot Encoding: Converting categorical variables into binary vectors, allowing your LLM to understand and process these variables effectively.

3. Aggregation: Creating new features by aggregating existing ones, summarizing data in a way that highlights important trends.

Code Example: TF-IDF Transformation

Explore feature engineering with TF-IDF using Python's `sklearn` library:

```python
from sklearn.feature_extraction.text import
TfidfVectorizer

# Sample text documents
documents = [
    "The quick brown fox",
    "The lazy dog",
    "Jumping foxes are quick"
]

# TF-IDF vectorization
tfidf_vectorizer = TfidfVectorizer()
tfidf_matrix =
tfidf_vectorizer.fit_transform(documents)

print("TF-IDF Features:")
print(tfidf_matrix.toarray())
```

In this example, TF-IDF transformation converts text into numerical features, creating a matrix of TF-IDF values for each document.

Feature engineering is like a master craftsman revealing a gem's brilliance—it shapes data into valuable attributes that enhance your LLM's understanding. By mastering feature engineering techniques, you empower your applications to excel in uncovering insights, making accurate predictions, and navigating complex data landscapes with finesse.

Key Preprocessing Techniques:

1. Text Normalization: Convert text to a common format—lowercase, removing accents—to standardize variations and aid in consistent analysis.

2. Tokenization: Split text into individual tokens, enabling your LLM to process and understand text at a granular level.

3. Stopword Removal: Exclude common words (like "and," "the," "is") that add little meaning, reducing data noise.

Code Example: Text Preprocessing

Let's explore text preprocessing using Python's `nltk` library:

```python
import nltk
from nltk.corpus import stopwords
from nltk.tokenize import word_tokenize
from nltk.stem import WordNetLemmatizer

# Sample text
text = "The quick brown foxes are jumping over the lazy dog's back."

# Tokenization
tokens = word_tokenize(text)

# Remove stopwords
stop_words = set(stopwords.words("english"))
```

```python
filtered_tokens = [word for word in tokens if
word.lower() not in stop_words]

# Lemmatization
lemmatizer = WordNetLemmatizer()
lemmatized_tokens =
[lemmatizer.lemmatize(token) for token in
filtered_tokens]

print("Original Tokens:", tokens)
print("Preprocessed Tokens:", lemmatized_tokens)
```

In this code snippet, we tokenize the text, remove
stopwords, and apply lemmatization to create a set of
refined and meaningful tokens.

High-impact preprocessing is like polishing a
gemstone—it reveals the brilliance within raw data,
enhancing your LLM's understanding and capabilities.
By mastering preprocessing techniques, you equip your
applications to tackle real-world tasks with precision

and efficiency, ensuring that they uncover valuable insights from diverse data sources.

Chapter 8. Model Compression and Quantization

In the ever-evolving realm of Language Model Applications (LLMs), efficiency isn't just about algorithms—it's also about optimizing the models themselves. This chapter unveils the power of model compression and quantization techniques, showcasing how they streamline model size, accelerate inference, and elevate real-world application performance.

8.1 Real-World Scaling Down: Model Compression Techniques

In the dynamic landscape of Language Model Applications (LLMs), model compression emerges as a strategic approach to downsize models without compromising their performance. Think of it as decluttering your workspace—eliminating unnecessary items while preserving efficiency. This section is a guide to model compression techniques, offering insights into how to achieve leaner yet potent LLMs for real-world tasks.

Why Model Compression Matters:

1. Efficient Deployment: Smaller Models, Wider Reach

In the dynamic world of Language Model Applications (LLMs), efficient deployment reigns as a strategic advantage. Consider it like choosing a versatile tool—you pick the one that suits various situations. Smaller models, resulting from model compression techniques, require fewer resources. This makes them ideal candidates for devices with limited memory and processing power, such as smartphones, IoT devices, or edge devices.

The Impact of Efficient Deployment:

1. Resource Optimization: Smaller models consume less memory and computational power, ensuring that

LLM applications run smoothly on devices with constrained resources.

2. Diverse Reach: With efficient deployment, LLMs become accessible on a wider range of devices. This democratizes access, allowing users to benefit from your applications, regardless of their device's capabilities.

3. User Experience: Applications that operate seamlessly on devices with limited resources ensure a consistent and positive user experience, fostering user satisfaction.

Faster Inference: Swift Interactions, Satisfied Users

In the fast-paced realm of LLM applications, user patience is a precious commodity. Think of faster inference like quick service at a restaurant—it keeps customers engaged and content. Compact models, achieved through model compression, contribute to faster inference times. This results in LLM applications that provide swift user interactions, ensuring responsiveness that aligns with modern user expectations.

The Power of Faster Inference:

1. Real-Time Interaction: Applications with faster inference respond promptly to user input, creating an environment conducive to real-time conversations and interactions.

2. Smooth Navigation: Quick inference leads to seamless transitions between pages or actions, preventing delays that can hinder user navigation.

3. High Engagement: Faster interactions lead to enhanced engagement. Users are more likely to continue using applications that provide swift and seamless experiences.

Economic Benefits: Efficiency Meets Savings

In the economic landscape of LLM deployments, making the most of resources is essential. Imagine a business optimizing its operations to maximize profits. Smaller models, achieved through compression, contribute to reduced storage and computational requirements. This translates into tangible cost savings, especially in cloud-based deployments where resources are metered and optimized usage leads to reduced expenses.

The Economics of Reduced Requirements:

1. Storage Savings: Smaller models occupy less storage space, resulting in reduced infrastructure costs, especially in scenarios with large-scale deployments.

2. Compute Cost Reduction: Lighter models require fewer computational resources, leading to decreased processing costs, particularly in cloud environments where resource consumption affects billing.

3. Scalability Benefits: Cost savings achieved through model compression amplify as your deployment scales, making efficient LLMs an economically sound choice.

Efficient deployment, faster inference, and economic benefits create a trifecta of advantages in the world of LLM applications. By embracing model compression techniques, you empower your applications to thrive on a variety of devices, offer swift user experiences, and drive economic efficiencies that contribute to business success.

Key Model Compression Techniques:

1. Pruning: Pruning involves removing unimportant connections (weights) from neural networks, resulting in a sparse architecture with fewer parameters.

2. Quantization: Quantization reduces the precision of model weights, replacing high-precision numbers with lower bit representations, thus reducing memory requirements.

3. Knowledge Distillation: Transfer knowledge from a larger pre-trained model to a smaller one, enabling the smaller model to mimic the performance of the larger counterpart.

Code Example: Weight Pruning

Consider weight pruning using TensorFlow's `tf.keras`:

```python
import tensorflow as tf

# Load pre-trained model
model =
tf.keras.applications.MobileNetV2(weights="imag
enet")

# Define pruning parameters
pruning_params = {"pruning_schedule":
tf.keras.optimizers.schedules.PolynomialDecay(init
ial_sparsity=0.50, final_sparsity=0.90,
begin_step=2000, end_step=4000)}

# Apply pruning to model
pruned_model =
tf.keras.models.Sequential([tf.keras.layers.InputLa
yer(input_shape=(224, 224, 3)),
```

```
tf.keras.layers.experimental.Pruning(pruning_par
ams), model])
```

```
# Compile pruned model
pruned_model.compile(optimizer="adam",
loss="categorical_crossentropy",
metrics=["accuracy"])
```

```
# Train and evaluate pruned model
```

In this example, weight pruning is applied to a pre-trained MobileNetV2 model, reducing the number of parameters and potentially improving inference speed.

Model compression is like packing a suitcase for a journey—it involves smart decisions to fit essentials while ensuring everything remains functional. By exploring model compression techniques, you empower your applications to operate efficiently across devices and platforms, providing users with responsive and cost-effective solutions.

8.2 Quantization for Real-World Fast-Track Inference

In the dynamic landscape of Language Model Applications (LLMs), quantization emerges as a powerful technique to accelerate inference speed without compromising accuracy. Think of it as converting a continuous spectrum of colors into a limited palette—reducing complexity while retaining essence. This section delves into quantization, showcasing how it paves the way for lightning-fast inference while preserving the precision needed for real-world tasks.

Quantization for Real-World Fast-Track Inference

In the fast-paced world of Language Model Applications (LLMs), quantization stands as a formidable technique that accelerates inference without compromising the integrity of results. Imagine it as condensing complex information into succinct highlights—a digestible version that retains the core essence. In this section, we explore the profound implications of quantization, illustrating how it transforms LLMs into agile powerhouses while upholding their ability to deliver precise real-world outcomes.

1. Inference Acceleration: Unlocking Speed and Efficiency

Quantization's first triumph lies in the acceleration of inference. Picture a streamlined car engine that delivers more with less—quantization reduces the precision of model parameters, allowing for simpler and quicker computations during inference. By representing values with fewer bits, the model's arithmetic becomes more straightforward, leading to swifter execution.

Understanding Inference Acceleration:

Imagine a deep learning model processing image data. Traditional models work with floating-point numbers that require complex operations. With quantization, these numbers are approximated with lower precision representations, making calculations faster and less resource-intensive. This acceleration translates to quicker results, enhancing applications' responsiveness.

2. Deployment Efficiency: Compact Models, Wider Reach

The second triumph of quantization is the optimization of deployment. Think of it as fitting a large canvas into a smaller frame without losing the artwork's essence. Quantization reduces model sizes, making them more compact and memory-efficient. This is particularly valuable in resource-constrained environments like edge devices or mobile apps, where limited memory capacities require judicious utilization.

Embracing Deployment Efficiency:

Consider an LLM that provides real-time translation. On a mobile device with limited storage and memory, a quantized model takes up less space, leaving more room for other resources. Smaller models also reduce bandwidth requirements during model updates, which is crucial for apps that operate in data-sensitive or low-bandwidth scenarios.

3. Responsive Interactions: Speeding Up User Engagement

Quantization's third triumph is its role in delivering responsive interactions. Imagine a conversation where every response is instant—a quantum leap in engagement. Faster inference achieved through quantization leads to applications that respond swiftly to user input. This immediacy fosters an engaging user experience that keeps users invested and satisfied.

Enabling Responsive Interactions:

Consider a chatbot app that relies on an LLM to provide real-time responses. With quantization, the LLM processes user queries rapidly, delivering answers almost instantaneously. This seamless interaction creates a conversational flow that mimics natural conversations, enhancing user engagement and satisfaction.

Quantization Techniques:

1. Weight Quantization: Reduces the precision of model weights, representing them using fewer bits. This lowers memory usage and speeds up calculations.

2. Activation Quantization: Applies quantization to the input data, further reducing memory and computational requirements during inference.

3. Post-Training Quantization: Quantization is applied after the model is trained, allowing for optimization without compromising the training process.

Complete Code Example: Post-Training Quantization

Explore the concept of post-training quantization using TensorFlow Lite's `quantization` module with a complete code example:

```
import tensorflow as tf
```

```python
# Load pre-trained model
model =
tf.keras.applications.MobileNetV2(weights="imag
enet")

# Convert the model to TensorFlow Lite format
converter =
tf.lite.TFLiteConverter.from_keras_model(model)
tflite_model = converter.convert()

# Apply post-training quantization
converter.optimizations =
[tf.lite.Optimize.DEFAULT]
quantized_tflite_model = converter.convert()

# Save the quantized model to a file
with open("quantized_model.tflite", "wb") as f:
    f.write(quantized_tflite_model)
```

In this code example, a pre-trained MobileNetV2 model is loaded, converted to TensorFlow Lite format, and then quantized using post-training optimization.

The resulting quantized model is saved to a file for deployment.

Quantization is like a magician who speeds up time, delivering outcomes quickly while maintaining the essence of the magic trick. By exploring quantization's facets, you empower your applications to be more agile, efficient, and engaging, enhancing user experiences without compromising on precision and quality.

Chapter 9. Hardware Acceleration in Practice

In the dynamic realm of Language Model Applications (LLMs), performance gains often hinge on hardware capabilities. This chapter delves into the power of hardware acceleration, demonstrating how technologies like GPUs and FPGAs can turbocharge LLM applications. By exploring real-world examples, we uncover how hardware acceleration elevates efficiency, speed, and responsiveness in the LLM landscape.

9.1 Real-World GPU Acceleration: Speeding Up with Graphics

In the realm of Language Model Applications (LLMs), speed is the golden ticket that opens doors to efficient data processing and real-time interactions. Imagine the highway—the faster you travel, the quicker you reach your destination. This section is a journey into the world of Graphics Processing Units (GPUs), powerful co-pilots that turbocharge LLMs, enabling them to process data at unprecedented speeds.

1. Parallel Processing Power: Orchestrating Multitasking Magic

Picture a juggler effortlessly managing multiple balls in the air—that's the magic of parallel processing, and GPUs are its grandmasters. These hardware wizards can perform a multitude of calculations simultaneously, unlike traditional CPUs that tackle tasks sequentially. This parallel prowess equips LLMs to take on complex computations efficiently, handling tasks like neural network training, complex data manipulations, and large-scale matrix operations with remarkable speed.

2. Data-Intensive Tasks: Slicing through Complexity

LLMs frequently grapple with colossal datasets, akin to sifting through mountains of information. Enter GPUs, akin to master sculptors carving through stone with precision. These computational workhorses are uniquely adept at managing data-intensive tasks. The parallel architecture of GPUs allows them to tackle vast amounts of data swiftly, making them ideal for processing large corpora of text, images, or other forms of input that LLMs feed upon.

3. Model Inference: Unleashing Real-Time Responsiveness

Imagine a live conversation where every response is instantaneous—that's the realm of real-time interactions powered by GPUs. LLM applications often require swift model inference to provide seamless user experiences. GPUs accelerate this process, ensuring that predictions and responses are generated in the blink of an eye. This capability is crucial for applications like chatbots, recommendation systems, or any scenario where user engagement hinges on rapid responses.

By leveraging GPUs, LLMs tap into a parallel universe of processing power, where multitasking is the norm and data-intensive tasks are handled with finesse. The real-time responsiveness achieved through GPU-accelerated model inference transforms interactions from laggy to instantaneous, delivering experiences that captivate users and establish a new standard for application speed and efficiency.

Leveraging GPU Power:

GPU-Accelerated Libraries: Seamlessly Boosting Performance

In the realm of Language Model Applications (LLMs), leveraging the prowess of Graphics Processing Units (GPUs) is akin to wielding a turbocharger for your engine. But how do you integrate this superpower into your workflow? Enter GPU-accelerated libraries, like TensorFlow and PyTorch, that offer a bridge to enhanced performance. Picture these libraries as skilled navigators guiding your LLM through the fast lane of computation.

1. GPU-Accelerated Libraries in Depth:

When you work with GPU-accelerated libraries, like TensorFlow or PyTorch, you're plugging into a world of optimized computation. These libraries are designed to seamlessly offload tasks to GPUs, tapping into their parallel processing muscle. This means that complex mathematical operations, which are at the heart of LLMs, can be executed with lightning speed.

2. Advantages of GPU-Accelerated Libraries:

- Efficiency Amplified: The beauty of GPU-accelerated libraries lies in their ability to distribute work across the multiple cores of a GPU. This parallelization unlocks the full potential of your hardware, translating into faster training times and quicker inference.

- Simplified Workflow: Implementing GPU acceleration doesn't require you to be a hardware expert. With just a few lines of code, you can ensure that your LLM benefits from the immense power of GPUs.

- Compatibility and Scalability: GPU-accelerated libraries have become the standard in deep learning. They're compatible with a wide range of GPUs and can scale across multiple devices, from a personal laptop to a cloud-based cluster.

GPU-Aware Data Preparation: Boosting Batch Processing

Data preparation is the foundation on which LLMs stand, and it's no surprise that even this foundational step can benefit from GPU acceleration. Consider it as streamlining your assembly line to produce more units in less time. Techniques like batch processing, where data is grouped into smaller chunks, can leverage GPUs' parallel capabilities for significant speed gains.

1. The Mechanics of GPU-Aware Data Preparation:

Batch processing, a common technique in machine learning, involves processing data in smaller groups or "batches" rather than one piece at a time. GPUs thrive in this environment due to their parallel architecture, which allows them to simultaneously process multiple items within a batch.

2. Advantages of GPU-Accelerated Data Preparation:

- Faster Data Loading: Loading and preprocessing data can be time-consuming, especially for large datasets. GPU-accelerated data preparation minimizes this bottleneck, ensuring that data is efficiently preprocessed and ready for training.

- Seamless Integration: Techniques like data augmentation or normalization, which are performed during data preparation, can be seamlessly integrated with GPU-accelerated libraries, providing a cohesive workflow.

- Training Efficiency: Faster data preparation contributes to shorter training cycles, allowing you to experiment with different model configurations and hyperparameters more rapidly.

By embracing GPU-accelerated libraries and optimizing data preparation through GPU-aware techniques, you elevate your LLM applications to new levels of performance. These approaches empower your LLMs to process data faster, train more efficiently, and deliver real-time interactions that set the stage for enhanced user experiences.

Complete Code Example: GPU-Accelerated Training

Explore GPU acceleration using TensorFlow with a code example for training a neural network:

```
import tensorflow as tf

# Load and preprocess data
# ...

# Define the neural network model
model = tf.keras.Sequential([
    tf.keras.layers.InputLayer(input_shape=(784,)),
    tf.keras.layers.Dense(128, activation="relu"),
    tf.keras.layers.Dropout(0.2),
```

```
    tf.keras.layers.Dense(10, activation="softmax")
])

# Compile the model
model.compile(optimizer="adam",
loss="categorical_crossentropy",
metrics=["accuracy"])

# Train the model with GPU acceleration
with tf.device("/GPU:0"):
    model.fit(x_train, y_train, epochs=10,
batch_size=64, validation_data=(x_val, y_val))
```

In this code example, the training process is accelerated using GPU acceleration with TensorFlow's `with tf.device` context manager.

GPU acceleration is like supercharging your car—it propels you forward with remarkable speed. By tapping into GPU power, you empower your LLM applications to handle massive datasets, process complex computations, and deliver real-time interactions that engage users seamlessly.

9.2 FPGA Fusion: Real-World Hardware Acceleration Insights

In the realm of Language Model Applications (LLMs), where speed and efficiency reign supreme, Field-Programmable Gate Arrays (FPGAs) emerge as the artisans of hardware acceleration. Imagine FPGAs as a versatile chisel in the hands of a sculptor, allowing you to carve tailored solutions that enhance your LLMs' performance. This section delves into FPGA fusion, shedding light on how these reconfigurable chips can breathe life into LLMs and usher in unparalleled acceleration.

Understanding FPGA Fusion's Impact:

1. Customization Unleashed: Crafting Bespoke Hardware

Imagine FPGAs as raw clay in a potter's hands—capable of being molded into precise forms that fit your LLM's needs. This customization capability is the secret ingredient that lets you fine-tune FPGA circuits to execute tasks with pinpoint accuracy. By sculpting FPGAs to match specific LLM operations, you extract performance that's optimized and unparalleled.

Understanding Customization Unleashed:

When you design FPGA circuits, you're not limited to off-the-shelf solutions. You have the power to tailor hardware components to your LLM's exact requirements. This customization can range from creating specialized processing units for certain operations to building custom accelerators that complement your application's unique characteristics.

2. Dedicated Hardware Acceleration: Tailoring for Efficiency

General-purpose CPUs and GPUs are like multi-tools—versatile but not always the sharpest for every task. FPGAs, on the other hand, don the cloak of specialization. They can be designed to execute specific tasks with remarkable efficiency. This dedication to a single task leads to faster processing and energy efficiency, resulting in a significant performance boost for your LLM applications.

Diving into Dedicated Hardware Acceleration:

Imagine you're building an LLM for sentiment analysis. By crafting an FPGA accelerator that specializes in sentiment analysis operations, you streamline the processing pipeline. This tailored hardware processes sentiment-related tasks more quickly and efficiently compared to a general-purpose processor.

3. Reconfigurability: Adapting to Tomorrow's Needs

Imagine FPGAs as ever-evolving tools that adapt to changing circumstances. Their "field-programmable" nature means you're not locked into a single configuration. As LLM requirements evolve, so can your FPGA circuits. This adaptability future-proofs your acceleration solution, ensuring that your LLM stays at the cutting edge.

Embracing Reconfigurability:

Suppose your LLM faces shifting workloads or algorithm updates. Instead of changing hardware, you can modify FPGA circuits to accommodate these changes. This dynamic reconfiguration allows your LLM to remain agile and responsive, even as it encounters new challenges.

Complete Code Example: FPGA-Accelerated Text Processing

Let's explore FPGA fusion with a code example that accelerates text processing using an FPGA-accelerated Bloom Filter:

```
import pybloom_live
```

```python
# Create an FPGA-accelerated Bloom Filter
bloom_filter =
pybloom_live.BloomFilter(capacity=1000,
error_rate=0.001)

# Add items to the Bloom Filter
items = ["apple", "banana", "orange"]
for item in items:
    bloom_filter.add(item)

# Check for item existence
print("apple" in bloom_filter)  # Outputs: True
print("grape" in bloom_filter)  # Outputs: False
```

In this code example, we utilize the `pybloom_live` library to create an FPGA-accelerated Bloom Filter. This showcases how FPGA fusion can enhance specific algorithms, providing accelerated solutions for LLM applications.

FPGA fusion is like having a master craftsman tailor a tool to your exact specifications. By exploring FPGA-based acceleration, you open doors to hardware customization, specialization, and reconfigurability, allowing your LLMs to evolve with the changing tides of technology while delivering unmatched performance and efficiency.

FPGA Fusion Techniques:
1. Hardware Design: Sculpting Customized Circuits

Picture FPGA Hardware Design as an architect's blueprint, guiding the construction of tailor-made circuits within the FPGA. This process unleashes your creativity, allowing you to craft specialized processing units optimized for specific LLM operations.

Exploring Hardware Design:

To dive into Hardware Design, you'll work with hardware description languages like VHDL (VHSIC Hardware Description Language) or Verilog. These languages provide the tools to define the behavior and structure of digital circuits. You'll design circuits that align with your LLM's computational needs, shaping

FPGA-accelerated tasks that are finely tuned for efficiency.

Use Case Example: Custom Matrix Multiplication Accelerator

Suppose your LLM heavily relies on matrix operations. You can design a custom hardware accelerator using VHDL to perform matrix multiplication with incredible speed. This FPGA-accelerated matrix multiplication unit seamlessly integrates into your LLM pipeline, offloading this compute-intensive task and boosting overall performance.

2. Interface Design: Bridging LLM Software and FPGA Hardware

Imagine FPGA Interface Design as a translator that enables smooth communication between your LLM software and the FPGA-accelerated hardware. This bridge ensures that data flows seamlessly, allowing FPGA-accelerated tasks to work in harmony with your LLM application.

Understanding Interface Design:

To accomplish Interface Design, you'll create well-defined connections that link your LLM software and the FPGA-accelerated tasks. This involves designing communication protocols, data formats, and synchronization mechanisms. The result is a clear pathway for data exchange that ensures FPGA-accelerated tasks become an integral part of your LLM's workflow.

Use Case Example: FPGA-Accelerated Text Processing

Let's say your LLM involves processing vast amounts of textual data. By designing a seamless interface, your LLM software can efficiently send data to FPGA-accelerated modules responsible for tasks like text parsing or keyword extraction. The FPGA-accelerated modules process the data swiftly and return results to your LLM software, all orchestrated through a well-designed interface.

By mastering FPGA fusion techniques like Hardware Design and Interface Design, you empower your LLM applications with a new dimension of performance. The synergy of crafting custom hardware units and seamless communication bridges results in LLMs that execute tasks faster, operate more efficiently, and deliver results that set new standards for real-world efficiency.

Chapter 10. Real-World Case Studies: Unveiling LLM Performance

In the realm of Language Model Applications (LLMs), theory meets reality in the context of real-world case studies. This section delves into two transformative scenarios—Revitalizing LLM Chatbot Text Generation and Pioneering Real-Time Language Translation. These case studies bring to life the strategies and techniques explored in previous chapters, showing how they are applied to enhance performance and efficiency in practical applications.

10.1 Revitalizing LLM Chatbot Text Generation for Real-World Speed

Imagine a chatbot that interacts with users seamlessly, responding with lightning speed and crafting engaging conversations. In this case study, we embark on a journey to transform LLM-powered chatbot text generation from mere potential to real-world efficiency. Let's explore how the strategies of parallelization, memory management, and hardware acceleration come together to breathe new life into this chatbot scenario.

Case Study Walkthrough: Enhancing LLM Chatbot Efficiency

1. Parallelization: Orchestrating Simultaneous Conversations

The chatbot landscape is bustling with activity, with multiple users engaging in conversations simultaneously. Parallelization becomes our ally, allowing the chatbot to tackle these interactions concurrently. By leveraging multi-threading and parallel execution techniques, we empower the chatbot to process incoming messages, generate responses, and manage user interactions simultaneously.

2. Memory Management: Navigating the Memory Maze

LLMs have an appetite for memory, and efficient memory management is key. We craft ingenious data structures that optimize memory usage, minimizing overhead and ensuring the chatbot's stability. Techniques like redundancy reduction and compact representations become our tools, allowing the chatbot to allocate memory efficiently while processing a plethora of conversations.

3. Hardware Acceleration: Turbocharging Response Times

To achieve real-time interactions, we tap into the power of hardware acceleration. Custom FPGA-based accelerators are designed to expedite essential chatbot operations, such as sentiment analysis or context integration. These FPGA-accelerated components work in harmony with software processes, resulting in responses that are crafted at lightning speed and delivered to users without delay.

Case Study Impact:

Imagine users interacting with the chatbot. In the parallelized landscape, the chatbot manages multiple conversations at once, responding to each user's input without any noticeable lag. Behind the scenes, memory management strategies ensure that the chatbot's memory footprint remains optimized, even as the conversations ebb and flow. FPGA-accelerated hardware components contribute to the chatbot's quick response times, ensuring that the generated responses are crafted swiftly, enhancing user engagement.

By embracing parallelization, memory management, and hardware acceleration, our LLM-powered chatbot transforms from a responsive entity to a real-time conversational companion. This case study highlights the practical application of the optimization strategies explored earlier, demonstrating how they synergize to bring real-world speed and efficiency to the forefront of LLM-driven chatbot interactions.

10.2 Real-Time Language Translation: Pioneering Real-World Efficiency

In the global landscape of Language Model Applications (LLMs), bridging language barriers in real-time is no longer a distant dream. Welcome to the case study of Real-Time Language Translation—a journey that showcases the fusion of profiling techniques, preprocessing strategies, and model compression to pioneer efficiency in the realm of language translation. Let's explore how these strategies come together to create a language translation engine that redefines the way we communicate.

Case Study Walkthrough: Breaking Down Real-Time Language Translation

1. Profiling Techniques: Unveiling Performance Bottlenecks

Our journey begins with a thorough analysis of the translation pipeline using profiling techniques. By delving into execution times and resource consumption, we identify performance bottlenecks. This insight serves as the guiding light, pointing us towards the areas that demand optimization.

2. Preprocessing Strategies: Refining Input for Precision

Before translation, we navigate through preprocessing strategies that refine input data. Noise reduction techniques cleanse the input, removing irrelevant elements that can hamper translation accuracy. Feature engineering extracts meaningful linguistic components, enhancing the quality of the translation process.

3. Model Compression: Shrinking the Footprint

To usher in real-time efficiency, we dive into model compression. This involves reducing the size of the language model while maintaining its performance. Through techniques like quantization and pruning, we create a leaner model that accelerates inference without compromising translation accuracy.

Case Study Impact:

Imagine a scenario where you communicate with individuals from diverse linguistic backgrounds in real-time. As you input text, the translation engine springs into action. Profiling techniques ensure that each step of the translation process is optimized, ensuring minimal execution times. Preprocessing strategies refine your input, resulting in more accurate translations that capture nuances effectively. And thanks to model compression, the translation engine delivers swift responses without sacrificing quality.

In this case study, we're not just breaking language barriers; we're pioneering efficiency. The fusion of profiling, preprocessing, and model compression techniques forms a cohesive strategy that transforms the language translation process. The result is a real-time language translation engine that enables seamless global communication, demonstrating the practical implementation of optimization strategies to pioneer real-world efficiency.

Conclusion: Harnessing Real-World Efficiency in LLMs

As we reach the final chapter of our journey through Language Model Applications (LLMs), it's time to reflect on the transformational strategies that have propelled these applications into the realm of real-world efficiency. In this concluding chapter, we'll revisit the strategies explored throughout the book and set our sights on the performance-driven future that awaits LLMs.

12.1 A Recap of Real-World Strategies

As we bring our exploration of Language Model Applications (LLMs) to a close, it's time to reflect on the real-world strategies that have illuminated our path toward optimization. Throughout this book, we've journeyed through the intricacies of LLMs, uncovering strategies that enhance their speed, efficiency, and practicality. In this section, we'll recap the key strategies that have empowered us to navigate the complex landscape of LLM performance.

Parallelization: Unleashing Concurrent Efficiency

The power of parallelization allowed us to orchestrate multiple tasks simultaneously, transforming LLM interactions. Whether it's a chatbot responding to diverse conversations or a translation engine processing multiple languages in real-time, parallelization has elevated responsiveness and user experience.

Memory Management: Crafting Efficient Resource Utilization

Efficient memory management strategies, from ingenious data structures to memory-reducing techniques, enabled us to navigate the challenges of memory hunger. LLMs that once demanded extensive resources now operate efficiently, delivering results while minimizing memory overhead.

Hardware Acceleration: Turbocharging Performance

The integration of hardware acceleration, whether through GPUs or FPGA-based accelerators, revolutionized LLM efficiency. Complex computations and real-time interactions became a reality, as specialized hardware units executed tasks swiftly, leaving a mark of speed and precision.

Profiling and Analysis: Unveiling Bottlenecks

By profiling LLM applications, we unearthed hidden bottlenecks and inefficiencies. Armed with this knowledge, we fine-tuned our strategies, optimizing critical sections of the code to ensure that our LLMs performed at peak efficiency.

Data Efficiency: Crafting Ingenious Structures

Crafting data-efficient solutions involved strategies like redundancy reduction and compact representations. These techniques not only reduced memory consumption but also streamlined data processing, enabling LLMs to handle large datasets efficiently.

Model Compression: Scaling Down for Speed

In the quest for real-time interactions, model compression techniques stepped in. By reducing the size of LLMs without compromising quality, we achieved faster inference times, enabling applications to deliver swift responses.

Conclusion: A Journey of Transformation

As we look back on our journey through the world of LLMs and optimization strategies, we find ourselves equipped with a comprehensive toolkit. From orchestrating parallel conversations to harnessing hardware acceleration and scaling down models, each strategy has contributed to the overarching goal of real-world efficiency.

The lessons learned and the insights gained extend beyond the confines of this book. As you apply these strategies to your own LLM applications, you become part of a community that is shaping the future of language-driven technologies. The journey continues, and the possibilities are endless as we embrace a future where LLMs thrive in the real-world, delivering speed, efficiency, and impact.

www.ingramcontent.com/pod-product-compliance
Lightning Source LLC
LaVergne TN
LVHW051328050326
832903LV00031B/3428